EPIRUS

EPIRUS

A STUDY
IN GREEK CONSTITUTIONAL
DEVELOPMENT

BY

GEOFFREY NEALE CROSS

Former Fellow of Trinity College
Barrister-at-Law

PRINCE CONSORT PRIZE ESSAY

1930

CAMBRIDGE
AT THE UNIVERSITY PRESS
1932

CAMBRIDGE
UNIVERSITY PRESS

University Printing House, Cambridge CB2 8BS, United Kingdom

Cambridge University Press is part of the University of Cambridge.

It furthers the University's mission by disseminating knowledge in the pursuit of education, learning and research at the highest international levels of excellence.

www.cambridge.org
Information on this title: www.cambridge.org/9781107458673

© Cambridge University Press 1932

First published 1932
First paperback edition 2014

A catalogue record for this publication is available from the British Library

ISBN 978-1-107-45867-3 Paperback

CONTENTS

INTRODUCTION

THE land of Epirus lay remote from the centres of Greek culture, entered late into its circle and contributed little or nothing to its achievements. One Epirot was indeed famous in antiquity, but if the name of King Pyrrhus is still remembered it is on account of his war in Italy against the Roman Republic rather than for his rule over his own countrymen, whose history has never at any period aroused much interest. Yet Epirot history has, I think, some claim to be studied, and in this essay I have tried to set out what is known of it from the time of the Persian Wars down to the Roman Conquest, with special reference to the constitutional development which was its most individual feature. The mere fact that no such account exists in English would not of itself justify this attempt, for there can be few who are at once interested in the subject and unable to read the work of Dr Klotzsch[1]— but Klotzsch and equally with him those who have dealt with the Epirot constitution in the standard text-books of Greek antiquities[2] seem to me to have misread the evidence afforded by the Dodona inscriptions and so to have left room for a further treatment of the subject.

To make a readable story out of the scattered references and the handful of inscriptions on which our knowledge of Epirus in antiquity depends has proved a task beyond my powers—and even such coherence as I have been able to impart to my narrative has only been achieved by a liberal use of conjecture based upon the course of contemporary events in parts of Greece the history of which is better preserved to us. It may be asked, perhaps, whether it was worth while to make so many guesses which must be suspect to the specialist where there was no compensating

[1] C. Klotzsch, *Epeirotische Geschichte bis zum Jahre* 280 *v. Chr.*
[2] E.g. Heinrich Swoboda in Hermann and Georg Busolt in Müller.

hope of attracting the general reader, and whether it would not have been better to have abandoned any attempt at continuity in favour of a series of separate articles. There is, however, a certain advantage in a continuous presentation, for Epirot history as a whole illustrates the truth, which still needs to be emphasised, that the Macedonian Conquest is no proper stopping-place in Greek history. So long no doubt as that subject is regarded chiefly as a useful accompaniment to an appreciation of the various achievements of the Greek genius there are plausible grounds for limiting the study of it to what is known as the "Great Age" of Greece, but if Greek history is to stand on its own legs as an independent enquiry the third and second centuries must be held to be as worthy of attention as the fourth or the fifth.

It remains for me to mention the names of some to whose writings or assistance I am particularly indebted. At every turn I have relied upon the work of the late Karl Julius Beloch—the rock upon which so much of our knowledge of hellenistic history is based. In the following pages I have emphasised—no doubt beyond their importance— a few points on which I have ventured to differ from him; it is, therefore, the more necessary for me to acknowledge here how often I have silently accepted his conclusions. To Dr W. W. Tarn I owe a double debt. His *Antigonos Gonatas* and the chapters which he has contributed to the *Cambridge Ancient History* have been of the greatest assistance to me, and he has himself taken the kindest interest in my work. Professor F. E. Adcock, who first suggested this line of research to me, has aided me throughout with his advice. Finally, I wish to thank the staff of the University Press for the help which they have given me in this my first experience of authorship.

G. N. C.

Lincoln's Inn,
April 1932.

LIST OF ABBREVIATIONS

Beloch = K. J. Beloch, *Griechische Geschichte*, vol. IV, ed. 2. Berlin-Leipzig, 1925–7.

Busolt = G. Busolt, "Griechische Staatskunde" in Ivan von Müller's *Handbuch*, IV. 1. 1, ed. 3. Munich, 1926.

C.A.H. = *Cambridge Ancient History*. Cambridge, vol. VI, 1927; vol. VII, 1928; vol. VIII, 1930.

I.G. = *Inscriptiones Graecae*.

Kaerst = J. Kaerst, *Geschichte des Hellenismus*, vol. I, ed. 3, 1927; vol. II, ed. 2, 1926.

Klotzsch = C. Klotzsch, *Epeirotische Geschichte bis zum Jahre 280 v. Chr.* Berlin, 1911.

Meyer = E. Meyer, *Geschichte des Altertums*, vols. III, IV and V. Stuttgart.

Nilsson = M. P. Nilsson, "Studien zur Geschichte des alten Epeiros", *Lunds Universitets Årsskrift*, N.F. Afd. 1, Bd. 6, No. 4 (1909).

S.G.D.I. = *Sammlung der Griechischen Dialekt-Inschriften* (ed. Collitz), vol. II. Göttingen, 1899.

Scala = R. von Scala, *Der Pyrrhische Krieg*. Berlin, 1884.

Schmidt = H. Schmidt, *Epeirotika*. Marburg, 1894.

Schubert = R. Schubert, *Geschichte des Pyrrhus*. Königsberg, 1894.

Syll.[3] = Dittenberger, *Sylloge Inscriptionum Graecarum*, ed. 3. Leipzig, 1915.

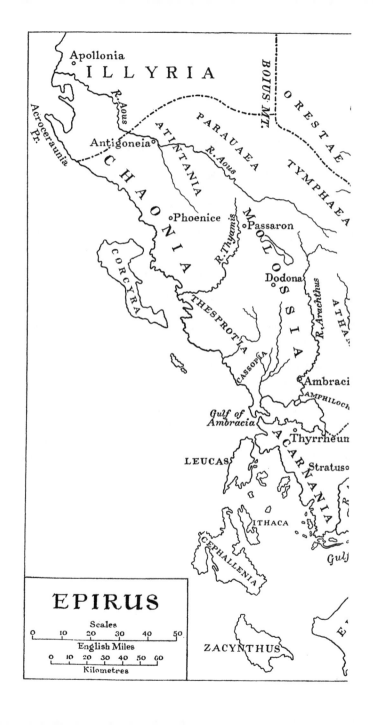

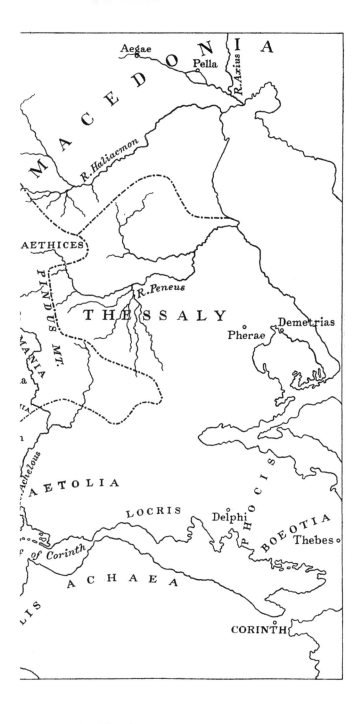

CHAPTER I

EPIRUS AND THE EPIROTS

IN antiquity the merchant sailing from Greece to Sicily, anxious to avoid the dangers of the open sea, followed the coast line of the Balkan peninsula to a point opposite the heel of Italy and then turned westwards across the Straits of Otranto.[1] A long stretch of this coast line—from the gulf of Ambracia northwards to the Acroceraunian cliffs—lay outside the frontiers of Greece as they were drawn in the sixth and fifth centuries before Christ, and all this region, the home of barbarian tribesmen, the Greek sailor of that time knew simply as "Epirus"—the Mainland—in contrast with the islands, Leucas, Corcyra and the rest, which lay opposite it. For a general geographical term to be applied in this way to a particular region is not so very unusual—for us, for example, the Peninsula means the Spanish peninsula—but in the case of Epirus there is this peculiarity that the name given by the foreigner came to be adopted by the natives themselves. In time the inhabitants of the "Mainland" developed from a group of separate barbarian tribes outside the pale of Greek civilisation to a united state within it, but they never found another name to describe their unity than that of "Mainlanders" or Epirots, so that the geographical term gradually acquired a political sense and the "Mainland", like the Netherlands, became the name of a country.

[1] The usual route was that taken by Aeneas—Virgil, *Aeneid*, III. 270–569. In the summer months it was not uncommon to cross from Corcyra to the Lacinian headland—Livy, XXXVI. 42—but the direct passage westwards from the mouth of the Gulf of Corinth was at any time a considerable adventure—Plutarch, *Dion*, 25.

The incorporation of Epirus in Greece took place in the course of the fourth and third centuries and is one instance of that general spreading of Greek culture and language beyond the old boundaries of which the hellenisation of the Levant in the same period is the outstanding example. It is with it, and in particular with the constitutional development that accompanied it, that this essay is chiefly concerned, but before trying to describe the hellenisation of Epirus, I should, perhaps, refer to a question which may seem vital to the subject and excuse myself for shirking it—the question whether the Epirots were Greeks by race or not. One might think that before speaking of the hellenisation of a people it would be necessary first to establish that they were not originally Hellenes, and that the problem of the racial origin of the Epirots—the subject of a controversy in which great names can be cited on either side[1]—would have to make its appearance in these pages. Fortunately this is not the case. For my purpose the ethnological truth about the Epirots is of little importance: it is sufficient to recognise the admitted fact that the Greeks from thinking of them, rightly or wrongly, as bar-

[1] Beloch, I. 2. 33, and Wilamowitz, *Staat und Gesellschaft*, p. 44, are in favour of an Hellenic origin, while Meyer, II. I. 271, and Nilsson, pp. 1–17, hold that the Epirots were of Illyrian stock. The arguments by which the controversy is sustained are mainly linguistic and their value is most difficult to estimate. My own view—for what it is worth—is that of the three big Epirot tribes the Chaones were definitely non-Greek (their name appears again in the form Chones among the Iapygians of Apulia who appear to have been allied to the Illyrians, cf. Wilamowitz, *op. cit.* p. 14), but that the Thesprotians and Molossians were essentially Greeks, members of the so-called Dorian stock which seems to have spread from Illyria over Aetolia and parts of the Peloponnese about 1000 B.C., cf. *C.A.H.* II. 518 seq. Subsequently, of course, they may have been contaminated by infiltration from the north. There is evidence to show that the Chaones stood in some degree apart from the Thesprotians and Molossians—Hellanicus ap. Steph. Byz. s.v. "Chaonia"; Plutarch, *Pyrrhus*, 1; Nepos, *Timotheus*, 2. See also Tarn, *Antigonos Gonatas*, p. 55 and the literature there referred to.

barians came in time to regard them as fellow-countrymen, and since a slight sketch of this change of attitude, in particular as illustrated by the use of the word "Epirus", may serve as an introduction to rather an obscure subject, I will give it at once.

The time at which Epirus became recognised as a part of Greece cannot be exactly defined, but we can confine it within fairly narrow limits. When Pericles sent envoys to every Hellenic state to summon delegates to a conference at Athens the north-western boundary of mainland Greece was at Ambracia, but a century later we find that this boundary has been extended to include the area between that city, the Acroceraunian headland and the Pindus watershed.[1] As with the country so with the people. To Thucydides the Epirots are barbarians, but in the third century they are everywhere recognised as Greeks and are among the members of King Antigonus Doson's Panhellenic League.[2] Meanwhile in harmony with this development we can trace another by which one among many "mainlands" becomes "the Mainland" *par excellence*, and the new Greek state gains the name that it has never lost. In Homer, where mention is made of the "mainland" opposite Ithaca, the use is purely geographical,[3] but when we read in Pindar that "Neoptolemus reigns over all the wide extent of Epirus with its upland

[1] Compare Herodotus, VIII. 47, and Plutarch, *Pericles*, 17, with Plutarch, *Phocion*, 29.
[2] Compare Thucydides, II. 80–81, with Polybius, IV. 9. 4. The Epirots were not members of the League of Corinth, but this does not show that they were not considered to be Greeks in 337, for there were special reasons which made their membership of that body almost impossible; see p. 40 below. Polybius, XVIII. 5. 8, gives the names of some other tribes which had become Greek by the third century, and shows that a distinction was sometimes drawn between them and the "old" Greeks.
[3] *Iliad*, II. 635. Cf. Rylands Papyri 18, where Beloch, I. 2. 279, thinks that it is the mainland of North-West Greece that is in question.

pastures that slope from Dodona down to the Ionian Strait",[1] we can see that the "Mainland" when applied to that particular region is already acquiring a capital letter, though its inhabitants were still no more than a group of barbarian tribes. To Greeks of the Aegaean, however, it might well seem that if any mainland was to have pre-eminence it should be the continent of Asia rather than any part of the Balkan peninsula, and so one finds at this time a certain conflict of usage which is well illustrated in a passage of Euripides' *Andromache*. Hermione accuses Andromache of having given her drugs to make her barren. "For", she says, "an Epirot woman ('Ηπειρῶτις) is skilled in such practices." Now Andromache was, of course, a native of the Troad, and so it is clear that Euri-pides is using the word Epirot primarily in its sense of Asiatic, but since the play was written with reference to the Balkan Epirus, which according to tradition became Andro-mache's second home, and since, too,—the Epirots had an evil reputation as poisoners and casters of spells—it seems likely that a *double entendre* was intended.[2] In the next century the gradual hellenisation and uni-fication of the country made it increasingly natural to limit the use of "Mainland" without a context to the land of the Epirots, but the great authority of Isocrates kept up the use of the word as a synonym for Asia,[3] and it is not until the age of Alexander that we can say that just as the Epirots are now Greeks so Epirus has taken its place beside Aetolia and Acarnania as the name of a Greek state. With so much by way of introduction, I will attempt to set out the little that is known of the early history and institutions of the more important Epirot

[1] *Nemean*, IV. 51. Cf. Wilamowitz, *Pindaros*, p. 401 n.
[2] Euripides, *Andromache*, 159–60 (*c.* 420 B.C.). See also p. 12 n. 4 below. Aelian, *Nat. An.* XV. 11. Robertson in *Classical Review*, 1923, p. 60 n. 13.
[3] Harpocration, s.v. "Epirus".

tribes, the elements of which the state of Epirus was to be composed.

Theopompus, writing at a time when Epirus was not yet a political unit, speaks of fourteen Epirot tribes, and Strabo, three hundred years later, while complaining that the ruthlessness of Roman conquest and the uniformity of Roman rule had all but obliterated the old boundaries, has preserved the names of eleven of them. Most, if not all, of these came at one time or another to be included in the state of Epirus, but its nucleus was formed by three tribes far larger than the rest—the Thesprotians, Molossians and Chaonians—and it is with them alone that we need at present concern ourselves.[1] The territory of the Thesprotians stretched along the coast from Ambracia northwards to the river Thyamis and inland to Dodona; Chaonia lay between the Thyamis and the Illyrian border which ran eastwards from the Acroceraunian headland; while the homeland of the Molossians was in the interior about the township of Passaron.[2] Of the three it was natural that the Thesprotians should be in early days the best known to the Greeks, for the mountain range of Pindus formed such a barrier against the traveller from the east that the Greek visiting Epirus would generally approach it from the south and the sea. Furthermore, the object of his visit was as likely as not the holy place of Dodona, where a little pocket of Greeks left behind in some early migration maintained the cult and oracle of Zeus, the sky god of the

---

[1] Theopompus ap. Strab. VII. 323. The other eight tribes mentioned by Strabo (323-6) are the Athamanians, Aethices, Tymphaeans, Parauaeans, Orestae, Atintanes, Amphilochoi, and Cassopaeoi. When Klotzsch (p. 10 n. 1) says that we know of many more than fourteen Epirot tribes he is reckoning in subdivisions of tribes which may never have existed as independent political units.

[2] For Thesprotia see Thucydides, I. 46, and Pausanias, I. 11. 2. For Molossia, Hecataeus ap. Steph. Byz. s.v. "Dodona" and Plutarch, *Pyrrhus*, 5.

Hellenes;[1] and the territory of Dodona was originally under Thesprotian control. But about the time of the Persian Wars the Molossians seem to have pressed down from the north, to have established a sort of suzerainty over the Thesprotians and to have taken their place as the masters of Dodona. When Aeschylus speaks of "the land of the Molossians and the oracle of Thesprotian Zeus" his words seem to express the change—the temple no longer in Thesprotian territory, but the god with a proper conservatism retaining the name of the former masters of his shrine.[2] The appearance of the Molossians at Dodona is an event of the first importance in the history of Epirus, for the

[1] The oracle at Dodona and its "personnel" were definitely Greek, Herodotus, IV. 33. Cf. Glotz, *Histoire Grecque*, I. 97, and Meyer, II. I. 269–70. Originally it seems to have been closely connected with the Achaeans of southern Thessaly, Homer, *Iliad*, XVI. 233 seq. and II. 681. Meyer observes that its cult at this early time differed considerably from the later forms which we hear of in Herodotus and Strabo, e.g. in the *Iliad* it appears as a "dream" oracle, whereas in later times Zeus spoke in the rustling of the oak leaves. Whether this change was in any way due to Dorian influence or whether the character of the oracle in later times was Dorian or Achaean it is impossible to say. At all events, Dodona formed a little island of hellenism in the midst of peoples which were considered—rightly or wrongly—as barbarian. For traces of a pre-Greek cult see Tarn, *Antigonos Gonatas*, p. 59 n. and literature there cited.

[2] The Thesprotians are the only Epirot tribe mentioned in Homer, e.g. *Odyssey*, XIV. 315. Strabo, VII. 328, records that Dodona was originally controlled by them but later by the Molossians. The first definite reference to Molossian control is Hypereides, *pro Euxenippo*, 36 (c. 330), and since Strabo (*l.c.*) says that Pindar and the tragic poets spoke of "Thesprotian" Dodona, and Herodotus, II. 56, couples the oracle with the Thesprotians, it has been thought that the change of control did not come about until c. 400. But the poetic use can be easily explained as traditional (cf. *Prometheus Vinctus*, 829–30, which I have quoted in the text) and Herodotus is referring to the foundation of the oracle many centuries before his own visit to Dodona. On the other hand, Pindar speaks of Neoptolemus as having ruled a Molossian kingdom which included Dodona, *Nemean*, IV. 53; *Paean*, 6. 109, and since he is at pains to emphasise that the hero's descendants are still kings of the Molossians, *Nemean*, VII. 39, it seems to me clear

closer contact with the Greek world which the tribe enjoyed in consequence of it encouraged its royal clan to put
forward the claim that they were descendants of the hero
Achilles and in this way to take the first step along the road
which was to lead to the hellenisation of the whole country.
The origin and history of this claim is of itself of some
interest and I need not, perhaps, apologise for describing
it in detail.

One of the many stories which dealt with the fortunes of
the heroes of the Trojan War after the city's fall related
that Neoptolemus, the son of Achilles, lived for a short
while among the Molossians in Epirus on his way back to
his home in Thessaly. Hitherto it had not been suggested
that Epirus contained any traces of his stay there, but it
happened that the royal clan which supplied the Molossians
with their kings revered as its original ancestor a certain
Pielos—a figure quite unknown to Greek mythology, but
one whose name bore a resemblance to that of Achilles'
father Peleus. This coincidence now enabled some in-
genious mind to put forward a story which made Pielos or
Peleus a son of Neoptolemus who had been named after
his great-grandfather and who continued his father's brief
rule over the Molossians. The intervening generations were
filled in with some dozen appropriate names and the reigning
monarch, whose own name was probably Admetus, appeared
at the end of the list as a direct descendant of Achilles.[1]

that they too must have controlled Dodona at the time when Pindar
wrote those odes, i.e. from about 485 onwards. In addition to gaining
control of Dodona the Molossians must also, I think, have exercised a
suzerainty over the Thesprotians about this time. Pindar speaks of
Neoptolemus' Epirot kingdom stretching from "Dodona to the
Ionian Strait" and of the hero having landed at Ephyra on the Thesprotian coast, *Nemean*, IV. 53 and VII. 38, I cannot believe that the
rule of Neoptolemus' descendants was less extensive. Nilsson, however, is not of this opinion (p. 21).

[1] For the history of the claim to descent from Achilles, see Appendix
I, p. 100. Eusebius, *Chronicon*, I. pp. 233-4 in Schoene's edition,

Without advertisement the pedigree might have had slight currency and little effect, but the dynasty was fortunate enough to secure in the poet Pindar a sponsor who spread a knowledge of it far and wide in the Greek world. Since there was little in the circumstances of the Molossians themselves to invite the attention of the laureate of the age, the guest-friend of the princes of Acragas and Syracuse, we may guess that it was Zeus of Dodona that formed the link between the poet and the tribe. Among the *Hymns* was one written in honour of the god, and Pindar himself may well have visited Dodona in connection with its performance, perhaps as a member of that mission of ceremony which his native Thebes sent each year to Zeus' temple there.[1] At Dodona he would naturally meet the leading men among the Molossians, but whether he met them or not the fourth and seventh Nemean odes bear witness to his interest in their pedigree.[2] The tribesmen did the little that was in their power to repay the debt, but the office of Molossian "proxenos" at Thebes can have meant little to the man on whom Athens had conferred a like honour in return for a single laudatory epithet:[3] to the Molossians, on the other hand, Pindar's aid was invaluable.

The hall-mark of hellenism was admittance as a competitor at the Olympic games, and sooner or later the Molossian kings must have proved their pedigree to the

---

says that Pyrrhus was twenty-third in the list. There were seven kings between Pyrrhus and Tharypas, and Pausanias, I. 11. 1, says that the latter was the fifteenth in descent from the hero. There were, therefore, about a dozen to bridge the gap from about 480 to heroic times.

[1] Only fragments of the hymn survive, 57–60 in Schröder's edition. For the mission from Thebes to Dodona, see Strabo, IX. 402.

[2] For Pindar's part in the origin and spreading of the Aeacid pedigree, see the scholia to *Nemean*, VII. 64, and Wilamowitz, *Pindaros*, p. 167. To say with Nilsson (p. 24) that that pedigree is a creation of the fourth century is to neglect the evidence of Pindar and Euripides altogether.

[3] Isocrates, *De Antidosi*, 166.

satisfaction of the stewards, the committee of privilege of
Greece. There is no evidence to show that they took part
in the games before the fourth century, but it is likely
enough that they were no later in gaining the right to do so
than the kings of Macedon whose descent from Heracles
was proved about the time of the Persian Wars.[1] Both
pedigrees, be it noticed, were in their origin confined to
the ruling houses. The Aeacids were "Thessalians"—
descendants of Achilles, a native of Thessaly—ruling over
barbarous Molossians, while the Heraclids were the off-
spring of the Argive Heracles ruling in Macedon over an
alien people.[2] But from the first the "hellenism" of the
dynasty furthered the hellenisation of the people, and when
in time the Molossians as a whole came to be considered
Greeks, all equally laid claim to the heroic ancestry which
had once been the privilege of their royal house.[3]

There is, then, some ground for saying that the hellenisation of Epirus began about the time of the Persian Wars,
but we have, of course, no material of so early a date from
which to trace a continuous history of the tribes in relation
to the history of the Greek states. Our whole knowledge
of the half-century between the Persian and Peloponnesian
Wars is notoriously scanty, and from Epirus there is but
a single incident preserved to us from it. It is possible—as

[1] Alexander the Phil-hellene of Macedon and the Olympic games:
Herodotus, v. 22. In VIII. 137 he gives a list of kings going back to
Perdiccas, who migrated from Argos to Macedon.

[2] Strabo, VII. 326, calls the Molossian kings "Thessalians" in
contrast to the "native" kings of the neighbouring tribes: Cf. Ἀχαιὸς
ἀνήρ in Pindar, *Nemean*, VII. 64, which refers to Pindar's royal host
and not to the Molossians in general. Herodotus, v. 20, speaks of
King Alexander of Macedon as ἀνὴρ Ἕλλην Μακεδόνων ὕπαρχος.

[3] Appendix I, p. 100. Herodotus, VI. 127, mentions "Alcon from
the Molossians" as one of the "Greeks" who were suitors for the hand
of the tyrant of Sicyon's daughter, but nothing can be deduced from
this passage, for it is to be supposed that such a man would have been a
member of the royal house.

we have seen—that the foremost poet of Greece was once the guest of the Molossian king: it is probable that within a few years that king or his successor received the greatest of Greek statesmen in his home at Dodona. When the venom and uncertainty of Athenian politics drove Themistocles into exile, and his enemies were so many and so powerful that his life was not secure in any corner of the Greece that he had saved, he is said to have sought the protection of Admetus, the Molossian king, to whom in the days of his prosperity he had refused some small request. Envoys from Athens and Sparta came to demand his surrender, but Admetus, with a primitive respect for the claims of a suppliant, braved their threats and assisted his guest to cross the mountain passes of Pindus, to reach the Macedonian sea-board and at last to find safety from his countrymen in the splendid shelter of the Persian court.[1]

Apart from this little incident, which seems somehow to have struck the imagination of the Greeks, since even after the lapse of eight centuries it is cited by a rhetorician of the Empire as an instance of the requital of evil with good,[2] we have no direct knowledge of Epirus between 480 and 430, but from our next view of the country—a view afforded by Thucydides—it is clear that these years had not been uneventful but had been marked by a decline of the Molossians before the rising power of the Chaonians, the last of the three great tribes. The homeland of this people lay—as we saw—to the north of the country between the river

---

[1] Plutarch, *Themistocles*, 24; Thucydides, I. 136. Meyer, III. 600, has suggested that it was at the time of the Leucas arbitration that Themistocles gave offence to Admetus. It seems possible that this same Admetus may have been Pindar's Molossian patron—the Achaean man of the 7th *Nemean*. Wilamowitz, *Pindaros*, p. 167, remarks that his name is appropriately Thessalian, but he also thinks—or thought—that the story that he befriended Themistocles is an invention, *Aristoteles und Athen*, I. 151.

[2] Libanius, *Epist.* 259.

Thyamis and the Illyrian border, but by 429 they had taken the place of the Molossians as suzerains of the Thesprotians to the south of the river and are described as exercising a hegemony in Epirus.[1] It is not probable that these successes were gained without fighting, but there is no trace of it in our sources and we are left in complete darkness as to the causes which may have made for Chaonian strength or Molossian weakness in these years. The occasion which prompted Thucydides to give his account of the various Epirot tribes was an attempt, made soon after the outbreak of the Peloponnesian War, by the Ambraciots who were allies of Sparta to overthrow the friends of Athens in Acarnania. To this end they engaged the services of a horde of neighbouring barbarians, and, since Epirus was at this time within the Ambraciot sphere of influence, contingents from each of the three great tribes and also from several of the smaller marched in their motley army.[2] But the attempt ended in disaster under the walls of Stratus, and when on top of this there came the victories of

---

[1] Thucydides, II. 80–81. From his account it is clear that the Chaonians were the chief Epirot tribe in 429. They are nowhere referred to before this time, and when Strabo, VII. 323, speaks of them as having ruled the whole of Epirus before the Molossians it is this fifth-century Chaonian hegemony that he has in mind. For him the Molossian hegemony is the later fourth-century hegemony dating from the reign of Alcetas, for he knew nothing of the earlier Molossian predominance which can be deduced from Pindar.

[2] The other tribes mentioned by Thucydides as taking part in the Acarnanian expedition are the Atintanes, the Orestae and the Parauaeans. The first—whose country lay to the north-west of the Molossians, Skylax, 26: Ps. Arist. Ausc. Mir. 136, were evidently in some degree subject to them. The Orestae who dwelt to the northeast on the other side of Mount Boeum, Strabo, 329. 6, are sometimes called an Epirot tribe, but are more generally classed as Macedonian; compare Hecataeus ap. Steph. Byz. s.v. and Strabo, 326, with Strabo, 330. 20. Robertson, C.R. 1923, p. 59, suggests that they may have recently broken away from the Molossians. The Parauaeans lived along the upper Aous due north of the Molossians: Plutarch, Gr. Quaest. 293, counts them as Molossian.

the Athenian admiral Phormion in the gulf of Corinth and the campaign of the general Demosthenes in western Greece,[1] the Molossians began to feel that an Athenian alliance might prove a means to regain their old position in Epirus. Acting on this impulse, they broke with Ambracia and through her with Sparta, and sent their young king Tharypas, who was, perhaps, a grandson of Admetus, to be educated at Athens.[2]

Their enterprise was well rewarded, for the Athenians were alive to the value of an ally in Epirus, and treated the young man with great respect. The citizenship was bestowed on him,[3] and care was taken that his illustrious ancestry, a source of legitimate pride to him, should be publicly recognised. About this time Euripides produced his *Andromache*—a play dealing with the fortunes of Neoptolemus and Hector's widow, who had been given him as a concubine after the fall of Troy. The scene was laid in Neoptolemus' home in Thessaly, and the plot happened to be taken from a version of the story which did not mention any connection between Achilles' son and the Molossians. With Tharypas in Athens this would never do, and so at the close of the play Achilles' mother, the sea-nymph Thetis, prophesies how the child of Neoptolemus and Andromache, the one remaining descendant of Achilles, will found a line of kings which shall reign over the Molossians "on and on in continuous prosperity".[4] Such

[1] Thucydides, III. 94 seq.

[2] Justin, XVII. 3. 11. Tharypas was "παῖς" in 429, Thucydides, II. 80, i.e. at all events not born much before 440. Perhaps he was a grandson of Admetus.

[3] *Syll.*³, 228, shows that Tharypas was made an Athenian citizen, but the honour may, of course, have come to him later in life. Nilsson, pp. 44–5, argues that it was bestowed on him at the time of the Corinthian War—*c.* 390—and that the story of his education at Athens is an invention.

[4] Schmid, in Christ's *Griech. Lit.* I. 343, seems to have been the first to notice the connection between Euripides' *Andromache*, 1243 seq.

a tribute, paid him by the most famous dramatist of Greece, must have sounded very sweet in the ears of the young prince who was himself the sole representative of his house, and we may well imagine that his reception in Athens made him an enthusiast for Greek culture, and that he returned home determined to confer its benefits on his semi-barbarous subjects. In antiquity, indeed, it was in his reign that men placed the beginnings of civilised life in Epirus. King Tharypas, it is said, was the first to bring order into the community by the introduction of Greek customs and language and civilised ways of life, while elsewhere we read of him as the founder of a political constitution among the Molossians, credited with the establishment of a "senate and annual magistracies" and the enacting of a code of laws.[1] But antiquity, I believe, was mistaken in assigning to him so important a part in the cultural and constitutional history of his country.[2] What we know of Pindar's Molossian patron goes to show that Tharypas' immediate ancestors were not so barbarous as Plutarch would have us believe, and that in the general field of "hellenisation" Tharypas himself can have done no more than further a policy which they had initiated. It remains for us now to approach the particular question of the Molossian constitution and to see whether Tharypas was in fact its founder and how, if he was not, it came to be thought so generally that he was. For this purpose

and Tharypas. See also Klotzsch, p. 221, and especially Robertson (*ubi supra*), who thinks that the play may have been performed at Dodona—see scholiast on line 435—as the "Archelaus" was at Pella. See also Appendix I, p. 100 below.

[1] Plutarch, *Pyrrhus*, 1; Justin, XVII. 3. 12. The "Θαρρύπαν πρῶτον ἱστοροῦσι κτλ" of Plutarch and the "Primus itaque leges, etc." of Justin may well derive from a single source, which one may conjecture to have been Proxenos—for whom see *Frag. Hist. Graec.* II. 461.

[2] Nilsson, pp. 43-4, agrees with me with regard to Tharypas, but puts the beginnings of the hellenisation of Epirus at a later date than I can accept in view of the evidence of Pindar.

it is, I think, necessary to give, in the merest outline, a sketch of the development of civil institutions in Greece.

The political unit in early times was everywhere the tribe. In southern and eastern Greece the tribal organisation had given way by the seventh century[1] to the "city state", which is commonly regarded as the characteristic Greek political form, since it was in a few city states in the two or three centuries of their primacy that the best of what has endured to us of ancient Greece was brought to being. But in the north and west the old organisation was maintained. In Aetolia and Ozolian Locris, and also, of course, in Epirus which, as we saw, was not a part of Greece at all until the fourth century, there never were at any time any indigenous city states.[2] When a desire for union at last penetrated these backward districts it expressed itself in federations of tribes which proved•more successful than most similar attempts in the more advanced parts of Greece, perhaps for the very reason that the units of which they were composed were themselves less unified than the average city state. But in the fifth century co-operation between the tribes of Epirus was still a thing of the future: as yet each formed an independent unit, of which we must now consider the composition.

In every tribe from very early times there was present in embryo the material alike for monarchy, aristocracy and democracy—the trinity which political science, faithful to its Greek founders, has until lately generally considered to comprehend all possible forms of government. Monarchy was there in the person of the tribal king who led his people in war and prayer; aristocracy in the form of the council of elders which assisted him with its advice; while the democratic element, at first very much in the background, was

[1] See *C.A.H.* III, ch. 26.
[2] There were, of course, Corinthian colonies on the coast.

represented by the general assembly of the tribe that heard and silently approved the decisions of its betters. But the tribal monarchy was not a monarchy by divine right; it was essentially a magistracy—a hereditary office which the tribe bestowed and which the tribe might take away or push into the background;[1] and it is a fact that from the beginning of our real knowledge of Greek history—that is from about 800 onwards—we see the kingship in a condition of decline. Even the epics—it has been said—offer us a "dissolving view of monarchy"[2] and a process of weakening, often ending in abolition, went on through the succeeding centuries. That the concentration of the people into city states contributed to this decline is generally remarked upon: it is not so often noticed that the same process took place, though more slowly, in those parts of Greece where the older organisation persisted, though the causes for it were very different. Amid the mountains of northern and western Greece a tribe that had entered the land in the stormy days of the migrations as a unity under a king would tend, once it had acquired a settled home, to split into a number of smaller divisions that only testified to the membership of the larger body by an occasional appearance at a tribal festival. Kingship, which in the more advanced parts of Greece could not survive the close contacts of city life, was hard put to it in the more primitive districts to retain such a measure of contact with the people as would justify its continuance. It is, therefore, not surprising to find that among the Epirots the Thesprotians, whose king is mentioned by Homer, were "kingless" by 429,[3] while the Chaonians had replaced their monarch by two annually elected representatives of the

[1] Cf. Wilamowitz, *Staat und Gesellschaft*, p. 57.

[2] *C.A.H.* III. 699. Cf. Bruno Keil in Gercke und Norden, *Einleitung in die Altertumswissenschaft*, vol. III.

[3] Homer, *Odyssey*, XIV. 316; Thucydides, II. 80.

royal house.[1] The Molossians, for their part, had evolved a procedure designed to set bounds to the royal power. Every year the tribesmen met together at Passaron, and there in the assembly of his people the king swore to rule according to custom while, in return for his oath, the people swore by the mouth of an elected representative to maintain the kingship.[2]

One might suppose that this would prove but a stage on the downward path and that the Molossian monarchy was doomed to the fate of the neighbouring kingships of the Thesprotians and Chaonians, but in fact it survived and prospered for two centuries to come and was the means to the unification of Epirus. We may attribute its survival to several causes. Something, no doubt, it owed to the prestige of its divine ancestry: much to the tact and caution with which—Aristotle tells us[3]—the Molossian kings exercised their prerogatives, but chiefly, I think, it was aided by a change in the attitude of the Greek world to kingship. It was in the fourth century that Epirus entered that world, and in that century—as I shall try to show with more detail in the next chapter—there was a reaction from democratic ideals which culminated, somewhat unex-

---

[1] Thucydides, II. 80. The fact that the annual "prostatai" of the Chaonians were still chosen from the royal family suggests that in 429 the abolition of the monarchy was a fairly recent event. Klotzsch, p. 9, has suggested that the Chaonian "prostatai" were copied from the constitution of Corcyra and that the abolition of the monarchy is a sign of the influence of Greek democratic ideas. It may well be that the reason why these tribal officers are called "prostatai" by Thucydides is that the Corcyraeans were the first to speak of them in Greek and recognised some analogy between them and their own "prostatai", but I do not think that it is necessary to postulate Greek influence to account for the replacement among the Chaonians of the primitive monarchy by these elected representatives.

[2] The Passaron ceremony is described by Plutarch, *Pyrrhus*, 5, and should be compared with the procedure at Sparta described by Xenophon, *Resp. Lac.* xv. 7.

[3] Aristotle, *Politics*, v. 9. 1313 A.

pectedly, in the hellenistic monarchy of Alexander the Great. The kings of the Molossians followed in the wake of their larger neighbour. While Philip consolidated the kingdom of Macedon and won a hegemony over Greece, King Alcetas and his sons united Epirus under the hegemony of Molossia. When Alexander of Macedon led the main force of hellenism to the conquest of the East, Alexander the Molossian led a smaller force to save the Greeks of Italy from their barbarian oppressors. Finally, in the age of the first successors of Alexander, King Pyrrhus attempted to set up in Epirus a humble imitation of the great hellenistic monarchies of the age. But through it all—and this is most important to be remembered—the Molossian monarchy retained the forms of its old limited character. In fact King Pyrrhus might be absolute, but in theory, whatever might be his position in his new capital at Ambracia or among the Greeks of Italy and Sicily, in Dodona and Passaron he was still the Molossian tribal king subject to the Molossian tribal assembly, and when at last the tide turned against absolutism with the rise of republicanism in third-century Greece, the old forms were used to establish that curious anomaly, the constitutional monarchy of third-century Epirus; as certain doctrines of our Common Law which had lain dormant while the House of Tudor ruled us revived at the touch of Sir Edward Coke.

"A curious anomaly" I have called it, and so, I imagine, the Epirot constitution must have appeared to Proxenos, the court historian, when he came to write the history of his country in the reign of King Alexander II, for it contained side by side a hereditary monarchy, an annual and elective magistracy, a council and a popular assembly. Such a combination, almost unexampled in the Greek world,[1] called for some explanation and this Proxenos seems to

[1] The only parallel of which I can think is Sparta.

have supplied by attributing it to King Tharypas who—he said—returned from his education in democratic Athens with ideas of annual magistracies and popular assemblies, and combined these institutions with the national monarchy.[1] In fact, however, the elements of monarchy, council and assembly were already present in the primitive constitution, while the germ of the annual magistracy is to be found, before the reign of Tharypas, in that elected representative of the people who received the king's oath and gave the people's in exchange for it.[2] In the course of time and under the influence of Greek ideas these native elements so developed that it was, and is, hard to see in the deliberative assemblies and executive officers of the third century the tribal meeting and tribal representative of the fifth, but the continuity is, I believe, real and provides a thread by which to follow Epirot history.

These few pages contain all that I have to say of the political and constitutional history of Epirus before the fourth century. It is little enough and much of it is conjectural, but, though details are almost completely to seek, the broad outlines of the position are tolerably clear. A group of tribes—barbarian, but coming more and more into contact with Greek civilisation. An occasional suzerainty of one tribe over some of its neighbours, but as yet no trace of the beginnings of a permanent union. In all the tribes a primitive democracy which, at the stage of development to which they have attained, is a sure hindrance to a coherent

---

[1] If I am right in supposing that he is the source of Plutarch, *Pyrrhus*, 1, and Justin, XVII. 3. 12. Cf. p. 13 n. 1 above.

[2] The annual magistrate of the Molossians—referred to by Justin *ubi supra*—appears in inscriptions of the later fourth and third centuries as the "prostates of the Molossians", the same Greek title as Thucydides gives to the Chaonian tribal representatives. It seems to me probable that his office originated long before that time in the ceremony described in Plutarch, *Pyrrhus*, 5, and that his original function was to represent the people against the king much in the manner of the "Ephors" at Sparta.

and energetic policy; but in one of them the tribal monarchy still in existence, limited indeed in its powers, but claiming descent from the greatest of the heroes of Greece, and destined to be the means of hellenising and unifying the whole country.

CHAPTER II

THE UNIFICATION OF EPIRUS

WE have seen that at the time of the Peloponnesian War Epirus was a region of undefined extent inhabited by a number of separate barbarian tribes, and we have said that in the days of King Pyrrhus—a century and a half later—the Epirots were a united people, living within definite frontiers and having some title to be considered Greeks. In this chapter I shall try to trace the course of this development, of which the channel was a permanent alliance of the tribes under the headship of the hellenised monarchy of the Molossians—a form of political organisation which Aristotle, towards the close of the fourth century, included in his list of "constitutions", and of which there is inscriptional evidence preserved to us.[1] Since the Epirots in this period were entering gradually farther into the circle of Greek culture it is natural that their constitution should reflect some of the current tendencies of Greek constitutional development and it is, I think, necessary for its proper understanding to notice the position in the political thought of the time of the two chief elements in it—the king and the permanent alliance or "symmachy". I propose, therefore, to preface this chapter with some remarks which may seem at first sight to have little to do with the unification of Epirus.

Monarchy—we saw—had so declined in every part of

---

[1] Aristotle, *Fragments* (ed. Rose), p. 313, Ἠπειρωτῶν Πολιτεία. This work did not, I imagine, treat primarily of the Molossian Constitution, but of the "symmachy of the Epirots"—the inter-tribal organisation the existence of which sometime between 330 and 297 is proved by *S.G.D.I.* 1336. See Appendix IV.

Greece that by the fifth century it was only on the border-land of barbary, among such as the Molossians and the Macedonians, that there was any effective[1] survival of it. But its disappearance did not mean that Greece was to be for evermore immune from autocratic rule. Most of the city states at one time or another in their history experienced the rule of masterful persons who overthrew established authority and sometimes succeeded in bequeathing their power to their descendants. Such occasional despotisms were not, however, in any sense revivals of the old kingship. The very name for them was different, and though the words "tyrant" and "tyranny" did not denote then, as they do to-day, a rule of unmitigated badness, there was always a flavour of illegality about them which had been quite absent from the old "Basileia". In this connection it is interesting to contrast the case of Rome, where there was only one word to denote personal rule, with that of Greece, where there were two.[2] In Rome after the expulsion of the Tarquins "Rex" was an accursed word—a title which no man but Caesar himself ever tried to assume and hatred of which contributed not a little to Caesar's murder: in Greece, on the other hand, "Basileus" was a title of praise, descriptive of a benevolent and constitutional rule, which the greatest tyrants might earn by unexampled services to the state. Thus Gelon, tyrant of Syracuse, was saluted as "Basileus" by the citizens on his return from his victory at the Himera which saved hellenism in Sicily from the menace of Carthage.[3] In the fifth century indeed, in the heyday of the Athenian democracy, personal rule, whether in the form of "kingship" or "tyranny",

[1] Both at Rome and Athens religious functions, which had been performed by the kings and could only be duly carried out by persons bearing that title, were performed in the republican period by official "kings" who existed for that purpose alone.

[2] "τύραννος" was originally a foreign word, apparently Lydian.

[3] Diodorus Siculus, XI. 26. 6.

was a rarity in the Greek world, but in the next century, which was marked by a pronounced hostility to democracy on the part of the intellectual leaders of Greece, there came a revival of interest in the idea of the "Basileus" which began rather as a theory of kingly qualities in private individuals than in an advocacy of monarchy as a political institution, but which in the long run had its effect on political issues.[1]

This revival can be traced back to the so-called Sophistic movement. It was a characteristic of the teaching of the Sophists to emphasise the importance of "personality" and to offer to their pupils a training in the arts of politics which would enable them to express their various personalities and thus to attain to the positions of influence in the community to which their talents entitled them. These professions were attacked by Socrates on the ground that the teaching offered was not such as would in fact best develop the character; but he seems to have been himself a believer in the possibility of a training which would produce better results in government than the haphazard methods of democracy, and to have bequeathed to his pupils the elements of a theory of enlightened rule. These elements were variously developed in accordance with the tastes and capacities of the different members of the Socratic School. Antisthenes, the "Cynic", laid stress on the labour involved in governing oneself and others—for him toil ($\pi\acute{o}\nu o\varsigma$) was the great virtue and Heracles labouring for mankind the ideal. Plato gave immortality to the conception of philosopher kings, and, to his eternal credit, did not shrink from an attempt to convert a real tyrant into an enlightened monarch. Xenophon shows the same spirit. Thus in his little essay entitled *Hieron* he introduces the famous tyrant in converse with Simonides, and

[1] See generally Kaerst, *Studien zur Entwicklung der monarchischen Idee*, and Barker, *C.A.H.* VI, ch. 16, section 1.

makes him give the customary democratic picture of the miseries of his position as an autocrat, while the poet, instead of agreeing with him and praising democratic equality, explains how he might convert his tyranny into a popular kingship. It is, however, in the writings of Isocrates, the greatest publicist of his time, that this philosophic monarchism comes into the closest contact with the facts of politics, and of him we must speak in some detail.

Isocrates was a man with no taste for profound thought, the master of an exquisite prose style, endowed with a self-conceit which knew no bounds and a perfect sense of the trend of the times. These gifts made him a teacher of great influence with a circle of correspondents spreading far beyond the political frontiers of Greece.[1] In his position he could not fail to contrast the unity of Greek culture and its powers of expansion with the political disunion which was the curse of his age. Let us consider for a moment the history of the first half of the fourth century. The downfall of Athens had left the Spartans in a position of supremacy in Greece—a position which they had so abused that within a few years they were forced to invoke the aid of the king of Persia in order to maintain it. By a shameful settlement—known as the peace of Antalcidas[2]—the Greek cities of Asia Minor which had been freed from Persian rule a century before were handed back to Artaxerxes in return for an arbitrament of the affairs of Greece favourable to the interests of Sparta. But even the support of Persia did not suffice to perpetuate the detested Spartan hegemony. On the field of Leuctra it vanished for ever, and any chance that a hegemony of Thebes might take its place disappeared with the death of Epaminondas at Mantinea a few years later. At this point Xenophon brings his "Hellenic history" to a close

---

[1] E.g. Nicocles of Salamis in Cyprus and Clearchus of Heraclea.

[2] From the name of the Spartan diplomat who negotiated it with Tiribazus the satrap of Lydia.

with the reflection that "after this battle there was even more confusion and disorder in Greece than before it", and the position was indeed depressing. No state was strong enough to dominate the others, but all entered with alacrity into a succession of small and aimless wars, while the Great King still ruled in Miletus and Ephesus, and Carthage seemed on the point of overwhelming the Greeks of Sicily. Yet, though the case seemed desperate, Isocrates believed—and was right in believing—that hellenism was strong enough, both in spirit and material, to push back its encroaching enemies and to expand beyond its old frontiers, if only union at home could be achieved. In the spirit of his age he tended to conceive of the unifying force for which he longed not as a state, but as a person—a new Agamemnon who should lead civilisation against barbary[1]—and such a leader he came to think he saw in a very unheroic but supremely able man, King Philip of Macedon.[2]

The history of the Macedonian people resembles in some degree that of the Molossians. There is the same doubt whether they were Greeks by race or not. They, too, dwelt just beyond the old frontiers of Greece and were commonly regarded as barbarians until at least the end of the fourth century; and with the Macedonians as with the Molossians the hellenisation of the people was preceded and facilitated by the claim of the royal house to descent from a Greek hero. We have seen already how soon after the Persian Wars King Alexander the Phil-hellene proved his Heraclid pedigree and gained admission to the Olympic games.[3] In the next hundred years a succession of capable—

---

[1] E.g. *Panathenaicus*, 76, and *Philippos*, 130–132.

[2] For Isocrates' political views and the question how far they contributed to or agreed with the settlement reached at Corinth in 337 see Wilcken, "Philipp und die Pan-Hellenische Idee", *Sitz.-Ber. d. Pr. Akad. für Wiss.* 1929, Phil. Hist. Kl. p. 291 seq.

[3] P. 9 above. Isocrates seems to have attached some importance to the Heraclid pedigree. *Philippos*, 108–9.

if unamiable—princes added considerably to the power of Macedon while all the time Greek civilisation spread farther among the people, so that by the time of the accession of King Philip in 359 the Macedonians were ripe to play a decisive part in the affairs of Greece. The situation there offered many occasions alike for forcible intervention and peaceful penetration, but not all Greeks viewed Philip's activities in the spirit of Isocrates. Many saw in him no new Agamemnon, but a barbarian who had come to destroy rather than to fulfil, and opposed him to the utmost of their power. Beaten at Chaeronea, they have had the better of the argument with posterity, for their case lives for ever in the speeches of Demosthenes; but whatever our sympathies, it is clear that the passionate hostility of so many Greeks to the establishment of the Macedonian hegemony made it very difficult for Philip to use his position as a means either to promote union in Greece or to bring the country into a relation of harmony with his own Macedonian kingdom. Among his advisers there were no doubt some who urged him to treat the country as several of his successors were to treat it,[1] to set up his partisans in power in every city, to put garrisons into the key fortresses to back them up in case of need—and to leave it at that. But Philip, though he did not neglect the positive side of this advice, was far too proud of his diplomatic skill—was, one may even say, too great a statesman to leave it at that. He wished to play, after his own fashion, some such part as Isocrates had cast for him;[2] he wished to have the co-operation of Greece in a war against Persia; and

[1] Notably Cassander and Antigonus Gonatas.

[2] It is not necessary to assume that Philip was directly influenced by any of the writings of Isocrates, and certainly the publicist was over sanguine in hoping that the king would pursue a Greek policy to the sacrifice of the interests of Macedon. But for all that it seems to me that Philip did take a far broader view than would, for instance, have been taken by Antipater, and I should suppose that in taking it he was

he made an attempt—the first of its kind—to effect a measure of political union in Greece and to reconcile the Macedonian monarchy with Greek republicanism. To understand the settlement which he brought about we must consider very briefly the nature of a "symmachy" and its position in the constitutional practice of the time.

A "symmachy",[1] which is the ordinary word for an alliance in Greek, means properly a combination to fight against someone else, and is very expressive of the particularism of city states that would not readily act in concert with one another except for the attainment of immediate military ends. There are, of course, examples in Greek history of "symmachies" which were more than temporary international agreements, of permanent confederacies with some form of joint central authority directing a common policy—but such organisations were in practice held together by one state which predominated over the rest and formed, as it were, a separate power within the confederacy standing apart from the other members. This dualism shows itself clearly in formulas such as "the Lacedaemonians and their allies", "the Athenians and their allies". Now these more or less permanent alliances—viewed as stepping-stones to political unity—suffered from two defects. None of them embraced all the cities, but each was limited to a few, so that they tended rather to ensure that wars were on a large scale than to promote hellenic unity. Secondly, although without some predominant power there could hardly be any prolonged concerted action at all, the pre-

acting on Greek advice—the advice, may be, of his friend Demaratus of Corinth, for whom see p. 41 n. 3 below. Indirectly, therefore, Isocrates may well have had a considerable influence on the settlement.

[1] See generally Busolt, p. 1310 seq.; "Symmachiai"—confederacies—must be distinguished from "koina"—federations—based on "sympolity" or "isopolity".

dominant member of these alliances tended to reduce the other members to the condition of cyphers. It is, for instance, a commonplace of the books that the Confederacy of Delos turned into an Athenian empire.[1] One might, therefore, suppose that there was a need for an organisation which should be pan-hellenic and not limited in membership, and in which the sustaining force should come from outside the body of city states; and that this was the need is, I think, suggested by the character of that "Peace of Antalcidas" to which I have referred.[2] That settlement dealt with the Greeks as a whole and, further, though executed by Sparta, it was imposed from outside by the king of Persia. Shameful it was, no doubt, for by it the affairs of Greece were submitted to the arbitrament of an oriental despot and in return for it the Greeks of Asia Minor were handed back to the rule of Persian satraps, but it reflected in some degree the needs of the time and was still the theoretic basis of Greek politics at the time of the battle of Chaeronea fifty years later. Indeed, the settlement at Corinth brought about by King Philip after his victory was regarded as taking the place of the Peace of Antalcidas,[3] and it was a corollary to it that a united Greece should undertake a war against Persia to recover Greek Asia and wipe out the shame of its surrender.

Our knowledge of Philip's settlement of 338/7 has been built up with great skill from two or three fragments of

[1] Cf. also the strictures on the interfering character of the Spartan "hegemony" contained in Isocrates' *Archidamus*.

[2] See Larsen's articles in *Class. Phil.* xx and xxi, where the analogy between the position of Artaxerxes in the Peace of 386 and the "hegemon" in the Peace of 336 is pointed out. Of course it cannot be pressed very far.

[3] Arrian, II. 1. 4, seems to show that the Persians considered the Peace of Antalcidas to be still in force at the time of Alexander's invasion. In fact it had been of little importance since the disappearance of the brief Theban "hegemony", but its continued existence lends some justification to Demosthenes' attitude towards Persia.

inscriptions.[1] The details of it are in many cases doubtful, and certainly this is not the place to discuss them, but the outline is fairly clear. After his victory the king of Macedon issued an invitation to all the Greeks to join with him in a "general peace"[2]—κοινὴ εἰρήνη—by which hostilities between members were to be forbidden and existing constitutions were to be maintained. To ensure the observance of its terms a council—συνέδριον—was set up composed of delegates sent from the member states in numbers proportionate to their ability to contribute men to a common force, and to this body was entrusted the duty of enforcing the "peace" against refractory states. Macedon—that is to say Philip—though it joined in the "peace" and swore to observe it in the same terms as the other members, did not send delegates to the council which was a purely hellenic body, but it was provided that the delegates were to elect a "protector"—φύλαξ—of the "peace" who was to be the "leader"—ἡγεμών—of the common forces when need for their use arose, and though their choice was in theory free it was of course intended and inevitable that they should elect King Philip to fill this position.[3] Furthermore, immediately upon its constitution the council entered into an alliance with the king of Macedon against Persia and appointed him commander-in-chief of its forces.

It is difficult to fit this pan-hellenic organisation into our constitutional categories. The common army, the power to intervene in the domestic affairs of member states and the fact that the council as a body entered into an alliance with

---

[1] Chiefly by Wilhelm, "Attische Urkunden," *Sitz.-B. Ak. Wiss. Wien*, pp. 165–6. Cf. also Schwahn, "Heeresmatrikel und Landfriede Philipps von Makedonien", *Klio*, 1930, Beiheft xxi, and Wilcken, *Alexander der Grosse* (Leipzig, 1931), ch. 2.

[2] In the sense in which the "King's Peace" was used in the Middle Ages. Cf. German "Landfriede".

[3] Schwahn compares the position of Napoleon as "Protecteur de la Confédération Rhénane".

King Philip, all point to a "Confederacy" rather than—to use a modern term— a "League of Nations", but on the other hand it seems doubtful whether the organisation itself was ever known as a "symmachy", which is often taken to be the nearest equivalent for "confederacy" in Greek.[1] But what it is important for our present purpose to notice is the extreme skill with which it was constructed—how adroitly it was accommodated to the tendencies of the age. It promised peace and union at home and made possible a war with Persia, while the Macedonian monarchy, without being imposed on Greece, was yet brought by it into a definite and more or less permanent relation to the city states. The great defect of the settlement lay, of course, in the fact that it was not spontaneous but was in effect dictated by a victor whose power was, and was known to be, overwhelming. Yet its merits were such that one may well think that with careful handling it might have been the means to a union of Greece within herself and with Macedon.[2] Careful handling, however, was the last thing that it was to receive, for Philip was succeeded within two years by his son Alexander the Great, a man cast in a very different mould from his father and one whose very qualities, to say nothing of his defects, unsuited him to play a cautious part in anything. It was the tragedy of Greece to have her Augustus before her Caesar.

In these few pages we may seem to have wandered a long way from the proper subject of this chapter, but I

[1] The pan-hellenic organisation seems to have been known exclusively as "the peace". The only "symmachy" was the alliance entered into by the delegates with Philip in his capacity as king of Macedon for a war against Persia. But in essentials the "peace" was what we may call in English a "confederacy", and I shall so refer to it.

[2] Wilcken (*op. cit.* p. 306), "Vielleicht wäre an einen gewissen Ausgleich zu denken gewesen, wenn Philipp noch dreissig Jahre regiert, und im Geiste von Korinth die Bundesparagraphen durchgeführt hätte".

think that the history of Epirus in the later part of the
fourth century may become a little clearer if one considers
the country as a sort of Greece in miniature with the
Molossian king in the place of the Macedonian. At the
time of Chaeronea King Alexander the Molossian was
closely allied with—and indeed dependent upon—King
Philip, and it is hard to suppose that the "symmachy" of
the Epirots under Molossian headship which seems to have
come into being at that time was not to some extent influenced by Philip's pan-hellenic organisation. Alexander
and the Epirots did not join in the settlement at Corinth or
in the Persian expedition, for they formed as it were a
separate entity and there was assigned to them a separate
task—an expedition in aid of hellenism in the West. There
was, indeed, one great difference between the two organisations, that Molossia was inside Epirus while Macedon was
outside Greece. Thus it was easy for a king of Molossia to
become a king of Epirus and in fact soon after Alexander
the Molossian comes Pyrrhus the Epirot, but no king of
Macedon ever became in any sense a king of Greece. Yet,
in spite of differences, to appreciate the position of the
Molossian monarchy in Epirus it is useful to bear in mind
the relations of the Macedonian monarchy to Greece; and
now we must return and pick up Epirot history where we
left it.

*   *   *   *   *

King Tharypas had been a friend of Athens and had
been rewarded for his friendship with her citizenship. It
would be natural to suppose that the collapse of the
Athenian power and the setting up of a Spartan hegemony
in Greece weakened the position of a prince who had made
alliance with Athens the keystone of his policy; and in fact
the first reference to the Molossians after the Peloponnesian
War shows us that by 385 Alcetas, son of Tharypas, had

been driven from his kingdom and was living at Syracuse.[1]
We do not know when he succeeded his father or when he
was forced to leave Epirus, but it is certain that during his
exile the Molossians were allies of Sparta[2] and it is possible
that it was the success of King Agesilaus' campaigns in
Acarnania in 389 and 388 that brought about a change of
policy in the countries farther to the north and the expulsion of a ruler who opposed it.[3] No king was set up in his
place, and it seemed that the Molossian monarchy had
suffered the fate of the other Epirot kingships, but Alcetas
was soon back on his throne again.

Two states dominated the Greek world at this time—
Sparta and Syracuse—and although there was an alliance
between them, a fugitive from the power of Agesilaus
could find no safer refuge than at the court of Dionysius.
Alcetas was especially welcome there, for the tyrant who
had already made himself master of the Greeks in Sicily
and had brought South Italy under his control, was in
these years aiming to establish his influence in the Adriatic
and Ionian Seas and thus to rob the merchants of Corinth
of that monopoly of the western trade routes which the
issue of the Peloponnesian War seemed to have secured to
them. Already he had founded a colony on the island of
Lissa and by restoring the exiled king of the Molossians he
might hope to gain a footing on the Greek mainland. The
restoration was carried out in 384 with the aid of a horde of
Illyrian tribesmen subsidised and equipped by Dionysius,

---

[1] The only reference to the Molossians which I can find between
Thucydides, II. 80 (429), and Diodorus, xv. 13 (Alcetas at Syracuse in
385, for which see Appendix II), is Pseudo-Andocides, IV. 4, which
speaks of an embassy to Molossia and Thesprotia in the earlier part of
the Peloponnesian War. This may, perhaps, indicate that the Thesprotians freed themselves from the Chaonians and followed the example of
Tharypas in friendship with Athens.

[2] Diodorus, xv. 13.

[3] Xenophon, *Hellenica*, IV. 6. 2—7. 1.

who also took the precaution of causing Alcetas to be made a Syracusan citizen and to be adopted by his brother Leptines.[1] The wisdom of this step was soon apparent; for when the Molossians appealed to Sparta for aid against their returning exile and his barbarian allies, the Spartans were ready to help against the Illyrians but unwilling to take any steps against a prince who was in some degree the representative of the tyrant of Syracuse. So the barbarians returned home and Alcetas was left in secure possession of his kingdom.

It is in the years immediately following this restoration that Epirus begins to emerge as a political unit under the headship of the Molossians and their king. In 429—it may be remembered—the Chaonians were the chief tribe and enjoyed a sort of suzerainty over the Thesprotians; but in 373 we find Alcetas exercising a control over the stretch of coast opposite Corcyra, which seems to imply that he was now the chief power in Epirus and that the Chaonians were in some degree dependent on him.[2] It has indeed been conjectured on rather fragile evidence that the connection between the two tribes was strengthened about this time by the marriage of Alcetas' son Neoptolemus to a lady of the former royal house of the Chaonians, and that the legendary genealogy which was being used to heighten the prestige of the royal house of Molossia was now extended by the addition that Helenus, son of Priam, became in his old age king of the Chaonians and was thus the ancestor of Neoptolemus' bride.[3] If the Chaonians were dependent on

---

[1] See Appendix II, p. 103.

[2] Xenophon, *Hell.* VI. 2. 10. Additional evidence of Alcetas' control over Chaonia is perhaps afforded by Nepos (*Timotheus*, 2) who says that the Chaonians were members of the second Athenian confederacy, for they do not appear on the list of members and must, therefore, if Nepos' statement is correct, have been represented by Alcetas and his son Neoptolemus, who do.

[3] See Appendix I, p. 100, and Kaerst, I. 176 n. 1.

Alcetas it is not at all likely that the weaker Thesprotians retained a complete autonomy, and it is at least probable that some of the smaller tribes to the north-east, the Atintanians, for instance, and the Parauaeans,[1] also came within his sphere of influence. But it must not be supposed that any tribe lost its identity or was amalgamated with the Molossians. It was only that among a number of weakly governed and backward peoples a man of ability and of some culture, backed by the power of Dionysius and at the head of one of the larger tribes, easily gained a position of predominance which justified the reference to him by a contemporary as "the chieftain in Epirus".[2] Epirus was not yet a political unit, but she was in the way to becoming one.

Meanwhile Alcetas developed a foreign policy. This— one might have supposed—would be directed for him from Syracuse; but it happened that a most unsuccessful war with the Carthaginians tied Dionysius to Sicily in these years[3] and caused him to leave his Molossian ally a freer hand than he might otherwise have allowed him. Left to himself, Alcetas, like his father, inclined to the enemies of Sparta who were at this time beginning gradually to raise their heads against the "system" of Agesilaus, and with two of them—Jason of Pherae and the Athenians—he entered into definite alliances. Jason, the tyrant of a Thessalian town, had taken advantage of the weakening of Spartan influence in northern Greece, consequent on the deliverance of Thebes from its Spartan garrison in 379, to use his great wealth and abilities to gain a headship over the other cities of the land and eventually to revive for his own use

[1] See chapter I, p. 11 n. 2.
[2] ὁ ἐν τῇ Ἠπείρῳ ὕπαρχος, Xenophon, *Hell.* VI. 1. 7.
[3] Diodorus, XV. 15, compresses the whole second Carthaginian War of Dionysius into the year 383/2. This is clearly wrong, but its exact length cannot be determined. The defeat at Cronion is usually placed about 375, Beloch, III. 2. 376.

the long extinct office of "tagus"—or leader—of the Thessalian League. His influence extended to the small tribes of the Pindus range between Thessaly and Epirus, and Alcetas beyond the mountains thought it wise to become his ally.[1] Meanwhile in 377 the Athenians had marked their revival by issuing an invitation to "all the Greeks and barbarians who dwell on the mainland and to the islanders who are not subjects of the king of Persia" to ally themselves with them "against the Lacedaemonians", and it is perhaps not too much to see in the express mention of barbarians as prospective members a hope that the restored king of the Molossians would be found true to his father's policy.[2] If this was so the hope was not falsified, for when in 375 Timotheus rounded the Peloponnese and appeared in the Ionian Sea with the first Athenian fleet which had been seen in those waters since the Syracusan expedition forty years before, Alcetas and his son Neoptolemus were enrolled in the list of members.[3] Hitherto Jason had hesitated to join the Athenian confederacy, but in the early months of 373 he was persuaded by Timotheus to follow

[1] Our knowledge of Jason's power depends for the most part on the account of it which he gave himself to Polydamas of Pharsalus, Xenophon, *Hell.* VI. 1. 4. He there refers to the Molossian king as his vassal, but he probably exaggerated Alcetas' dependence on him, Klotzsch, p. 46.

[2] *Sylloge*, 147; Diodorus, xv. 36. 5. "Mainland" is here used of the whole Balkan peninsula as opposed to the islands. Subjects of the king of Persia were excepted in deference to the Peace of Antalcidas.

[3] It is to be noted that the alliance is between Athens and the two princes, Alcetas and Neoptolemus; no tribes are mentioned. It would be interesting to know how many tribes they represented. Nepos says that Timotheus "socios adjunxit Epirotas, Athamanas, Chaonas omnesque eas gentes quae mare illud adjacent". "Epirotae"—a vague term—presumably includes at least the Molossians and Thesprotians. The Athamanians dwelt far inland and seem to have been quite independent in 395 (Diodorus, XIV. 82. 7) and 355 (*ibid*. XVI. 29. 1). If Nepos is right, and Alcetas represented them in the confederacy, his power in North-West Greece must have been more extensive than that of any Molossian king before Pyrrhus.

his ally's example,[1] and both princes soon had an opportunity of proving their value as members.

The chief among the allies gained by Timotheus in 375 and the corner-stone of the confederacy in the Ionian Sea was the island Corcyra. In 373 it was being besieged by a Spartan force and though in theory its relief should have been easy for a navy whose strength on paper was far greater than that of any fleet which Sparta and her allies could put on the sea, lack of money, which became the chronic malady of the confederacy, delayed its start. Corcyra would have fallen if the alliance with Jason and Alcetas had not made it possible to march a relief force overland through the mountains of central Greece and to slip it by night across the narrow channel between the island and the mainland.[2] Its arrival put fresh heart into the defence and by the end of the summer Corcyra was out of danger. At Athens, however, in the meantime indignation at the persistent delay of the fleet led to Timotheus being replaced in his command by Iphicrates and prosecuted for malversation by the politician Callistratus. His trial came on in November and so strong was the feeling against him that nothing but the support of Jason and Alcetas saved his life. The two princes paid him the unexampled honour of appearing in person at Athens to plead for him and the service which they had just done the con-

---

[1] In the matter of Jason's membership of the confederacy I follow Marshall (*Second Athenian Confederacy*, Cambridge, 1905, p. 68) rather than Beloch (III. 2. 158).

[2] There is no doubt that Alcetas was responsible for the relief force reaching Corcyra—Xenophon, VI. 2. 10—but if Beloch is right in saying that these troops were previously at Zacynthus—Diodorus, XV. 46. 3—Jason cannot have been of any assistance in connection with them. But I think that Xenophon (*ubi supra*) and Diodorus, XV. 46. 3, both imply that they were sent from Athens, and in this case Jason's entry into the confederacy in the spring of 373 made their march across central Greece possible.

federacy made it hard to refuse them.[1] There was, more-over, an additional reason for avoiding giving offence to Alcetas, and to explain it we must go back a little.

When the Spartans decided to attack Corcyra they told their ally Dionysius of their intention and suggested that he might help them. The tyrant of Syracuse had no desire to engage in active war with Athens and her confederacy, but since he was now at peace with Carthage and free to renew his interest in the Adriatic and the Ionian Seas, he was very willing to attempt to acquire Corcyra for himself. With this object he sent out a small force of ten warships loaded with offerings to Apollo of Delphi so that his admiral might adopt a warlike or peaceful attitude as occasion demanded. This squadron arrived off Corcyra about September when the Spartans had already retired; but by this time Iphicrates had managed to overcome the difficulties which defeated Timotheus and had himself reached the island with his much larger fleet some days before. It was not unreasonable for him to view the Syracusan ships as a force sent to help the Spartans and to use the gold and silver which he found on board them to pay his rowers; but Dionysius, of course, took up the position that Iphicrates was a sacrilegious pirate, and complained of him to the Athenians through the king of the Molossians. Thus Alcetas came to Athens in November 373 on a double mission—to defend Timotheus and to complain of Iphicrates. In this latter capacity he was more or less an envoy of Dionysius, and it was therefore as "Alcetas, son of Leptines, the Syracusan" that he accepted the honour of a crown which the assembly voted him.[2] We do not know what satisfaction the Athenians afforded Dionysius; but since

[1] (Demosthenes) c. Timotheum, 22; Xenophon, Hell. VI. 2; Diodorus, XV. 45–7. The only certain date is that of Timotheus' trial—November 373—and the relation of the other events to it is much disputed. See Appendix II, p. 105.
[2] See Appendix II.

within a few years they resumed friendly relations and even made an alliance with him,[1] it seems probable that Alcetas was as successful in this part of his mission as in the other.

This visit to Athens is his last that we hear of King Alcetas, and with him Epirus disappears from history for about twelve years. They were years which saw the decline of every power which Alcetas had known and the rise of none to take their place. The last traces of Spartan supremacy vanished on the field of Leuctra. The Thessalian power of Jason of Pherae died with him. Dionysius, it is true, handed on his empire to his son, but the vanity and incompetence which baffled Plato were fast dissipating their inheritance. Even the Athenian confederacy lost all influence in the West when Corcyra left it.[2] This general decay freed the kings of the Molossians from dependence on any Greek state, but left them to defend their half-civilised country unaided against attack from the north where Bardylis, an Illyrian chieftain, had built up a barbarian power which was a menace alike to Epirus and to the neighbouring kingdom of Macedon.[3] Hitherto there seem to have been no relations either of enmity or friendship between the Epirots and the Macedonians, but from this time onwards the histories of the two peoples are closely linked together.

Alcetas had been succeeded by his eldest son Neoptolemus, but the younger son Arybbas soon forced his brother to share the throne with him, and when Neoptolemus died about 360, leaving an infant son and two daughters, the uncle married the elder of his nieces and reigned as sole king.[4] Fear of the Illyrians drew him

---

[1] *Syll.*[3], 159 and 163.
[2] Diodorus, XV. 95. 3; Aeneas Tacticus, XI. 13.
[3] Frontinus, II. 5. 19; Diodorus, XVI. 4; Lucian, *Macrobioi*, 10.
[4] Pausanias, I. 11. 3; Justin, VII. 6. 10; Plutarch, *Pyrrhus*, I. Neoptolemus was dead before Olympias' marriage in 357, Plutarch,

into an alliance with Macedon, and after King Philip's victory over Bardylis in 358 Arybbas consented to his marriage with his wife's sister, the princess Olympias. It was a fateful union. The issue of it was Alexander the Great; it inaugurated a connection between Epirus and Macedon which in the long run proved ruinous to the smaller country; and almost at once it brought disaster on Arybbas. In the words of a contemporary, "never had Europe produced such a man as Philip the son of Amyntas",[1] and soon Demosthenes in the assembly at Athens was giving a lively description of the course of his energy through the stagnant waters of Greek politics.[2] "First he seized Amphipolis, then Pydna, then Potidaea, next Methone and then he came down on Thessaly; dealt with Pherae, Pagasae and Magnesia just as he liked, and was off against Thrace. There he set up some kings and pulled down others, but weakened them all, and when he came back did not turn aside to rest but undertook at once his war with the Olynthians, to say nothing of his campaigns against the Illyrians, the Paeonians and Arybbas." We see, then, that within a few years of his marriage Philip was at war with his wife's uncle.[3] One outcome of their conflict seems to have been that the Atintanians and Parauaeans freed themselves from any dependence on the Molossians.[4]

Alexander, 2: on the other hand, his son Alexander the Molossian was not born before 363, Justin, VIII. 6. 7.

[1] Theopompus ap. Polybium, VIII. 9.

[2] Demosthenes, *Olynthian*, I. 13.

[3] The exact date of Philip's first campaign in Epirus is in dispute. It is evidently about 352: Beloch, III. 2. 282.

[4] In 429 Atintania had been connected with Molossia—Thucydides, II. 80—but at the time of *S.G.D.I.* 1336, which lies between 330 and 297, the country was outside the borders of the Epirot league. Arybbas' war with Bardylis, whose kingdom lay to the north of Atintania, seems to imply that the district was still connected with Epirus about 359. It seems, therefore, likely that it detached itself after Philip's campaign. It appears to have been connected with Macedon in 314:

Another was that the little prince Alexander, son of Neoptolemus, was taken away from Dodona to be brought up at the Macedonian court; for the boy had a better right than Arybbas to the Molossian throne, and Olympias feared that he might not be safe in his uncle's hands.[1] Ten years later, when Alexander was grown up, Philip made use of his claim, invaded Epirus with a power that was not to be resisted and drove Arybbas and his family to take refuge in Athens. It seems that in these last years a mutual fear of Macedon had led to a renewal of the ties which had existed in the time of Alcetas, and now the Athenians received the exile kindly and voted that "the citizenship given to his father and his grandfather be confirmed to him and his children... and that the Generals see to it that Arybbas and his sons recover their kingdom".[2] This final direction was not obeyed, and it was without the help of Athens that the restoration one day came about.

Meanwhile Alexander became king of the Molossians, and Philip, who was fond of his brother-in-law—rumour which never spared him said too fond[3]—made good the loss of the Atintanians and Parauaeans by adding to Epirus the district of Cassopia to the south, with its Greek cities of Pandosia, Bucheta and Elaea.[4] His influence can also be traced in the constitution of the country, for the alliance of tribes under the headship of the Molossian king, which had probably existed in a loose form since the days of Alcetas, seems to have been organised at this time as the "symmachy of the Epirots"; and it is hard not to see here a link

Diodorus, XIX. 67. 6. Parauaea was Macedonian in 295—see p. 59 below—and in view of its geographical position cannot have preserved its independence longer than Atintania. With Parauaea probably went Tymphaea also.   [1] Justin, VIII. 6. 5.

[2] *Syll.*[3], 228. Diodorus, XVI. 72. 1, seems to be a year out—Beloch, III. 2. 292—and is certainly wrong in putting Arybbas' death in 343/2. See Justin, VII. 6. 12 and p. 43 n. 2 below.

[3] Justin, VIII. 6. 5.   [4] Demosthenes, VII. 32.

with the pan-hellenic organisation which was coming into being under Philip's auspices in these very years.[1] The Epirots did not send deputies to Corinth,[2] partly because the quality of their hellenism was uncertain, but chiefly, no doubt, because no place could have been found for the Molossian monarchy in Philip's league. Instead Epirus became a Greece in miniature with a king and symmachy of its own. The Epirot tribes, like the cities of Greece, continued to have their own assemblies and enjoyed a local autonomy, but all sent delegates to a council at Dodona presided over by the "prostates" of the Molossians, who combined this function with his presidency of the Molossian tribal assembly. Alexander's kingship, too, was still limited to his own tribe—he is always "the Molossian", never "the Epirot"—but he was, if one may borrow an expression from Corinth, "hegemon" of the Epirot confederacy and destined to lead it—as Philip hoped to lead the Greeks—on an expedition in the cause of hellenism.

The settlement of Corinth was intended as a preliminary to an expedition into Asia Minor to recover what had been surrendered to Persia at the Peace of Antalcidas. The "symmachy" of the Epirots was faced with an analogous task, another necessary labour in the cause of hellenism. The break up of the empire of Dionysius of Syracuse had been followed, both in Italy and Sicily, by an onrush of barbary great enough to fill Plato with despair for Greek civilisation in the West.[3] The lesser danger,

[1] The "symmachy of the Epirots" of *S.G.D.I.* 1336 is, I think, the "Epirot constitution" of Aristotle, and it seems to me very likely that it was first organised in the reign of Alexander in imitation of Philip's settlement at Corinth.

[2] The Epirots do not appear as members of the "Peace" of 337 in *I.G.* II². 1. 236, which contains a number of names from North-West Greece. The fragmentary condition of the inscription makes it inadequate to prove the point, but on general grounds it is exceedingly unlikely that they were members. Cf. Beloch, III. 1. 576 n.

[3] Plato, *Ep.* VIII. 353 A.

that from Carthage in Sicily,[1] had been already averted by the enterprise of Timoleon of Corinth, but in Italy the native tribes of the interior, the Lucanians and the Samnites, were pressing steadily nearer and nearer to the Greek cities on the coast. A few years before, King Archidamus of Sparta—son of the great Agesilaus—had led a mercenary force in answer to an appeal from Tarentum, and had laid down his life on the field of Mandonion on the very day of Chaeronea. Now Philip was supreme in Greece, and the appeal was to him.[2] Among his advisers were two Corinthians—Demaratus and Deinarchus—who had personal knowledge of the gravity of the position, and it was perhaps on their suggestion that it was arranged that Alexander the Molossian should lead the Epirots to Italy, while Philip led the Greeks to the invasion of Asia.[3] As a final favour on the eve of the two expeditions the king of Macedon offered his brother-in-law the hand of his daughter Cleopatra. The marriage was celebrated at Aegae, and there, in the midst of the festivities, King Philip was assassinated—at the instance, men said, of his discarded wife. At the time his death seemed to be politically of little importance, for the new king, Alexander of Macedon, proved well able to maintain his father's position both at home and in Greece, and in the spring of 334 was ready to proceed to the invasion of the Persian Empire. In the same year his uncle and namesake of Molossia crossed the Adriatic; but the two Alexanders met very different fates.

[1] The fact that the Carthaginian menace was really not so great as the Italian is brought out by Rosenberg, *G. der Röm. Republik*, p. 35.

[2] It is usual to say that the Tarentines appealed directly to Alexander the Molossian—e.g. Beloch, III. 1. 596—but the past history of Epirus gave them no particular reason for supposing that help would be forthcoming from that country, and in the circumstances of the time I cannot but think that the appeal would have been to Philip at Corinth.

[3] Demaratus and Deinarchus: Plutarch, *Timoleon*, 21, 24 and 27; *Alexander*, 9.

One died in his palace at Babylon, master of the world, while the other was killed in a skirmish somewhere among the hills of Calabria, betrayed by his allies and worsted by the barbarians whom he had come to conquer.

The little that is known of the Italian campaign of King Alexander the Molossian lies outside the scope of this chapter, but his death is an event of great importance in the history of his country, for the circumstance that he died childless[1] raised a problem of succession which could only be solved by the temporary extinction of national independence. In Molossia—as generally in the so-called "heroic" monarchies—the choice of a king rested in theory with the people, but natural conservatism tended to establish the ordinary rules of hereditary succession. Since Alexander had no brothers, in normal times Arybbas, his uncle and the husband of his elder sister Troas, would have returned to the throne; but in 330 there could be no thought of recalling enemies of Macedon from their exile and, therefore, the crown passed through the late king's younger sister Olympias to her son Alexander the Great. Epirus was thus incorporated in the Macedonian Empire, and the union, which lasted for some seven years, led inevitably to the formation of two hostile parties in the land— the one contented with the Macedonian connection, the other anxious for the restoration of the national monarchy. Since it was in fact a purely Molossian monarchy and its predominance in Epirus as a whole a growth of the last fifty years, one may guess that the "national" party was in the main Molossian and that other Epirots did not resent incorporation in a world-wide empire.

In 330 Alexander the Great had more to do than to con-

---

[1] It is generally supposed that Alexander left a child by Cleopatra. In Appendix III I have given some reasons for thinking that probably he died without issue and that, in any case, any child of his was dead at latest by 325.

cern himself with his inheritance in Epirus; but Olympias was glad of an opportunity to leave Macedon and be free from the control of Antipater, whom her son had left at home as regent. She seems to have moved from Pella to Dodona soon after her brother's death and to have considered herself as queen of Molossia.[1] No doubt she was left a free hand there, but officially Epirus was added to Antipater's governorship, and remained part of it until the death of Alexander the Great—an event which spread confusion from India to the Adriatic Sea and involved Epirus, as a part of the Empire, in the general chaos. The complications of the next twenty-four years of Epirot history are in many cases reflections of the complexity of the political situation in Asia and in consequence it is difficult to give an account of them without pressing a little way into the labyrinth of conflict and intrigue which stretched over the whole Empire.

At the news of Alexander's death many of the Greek states rose in revolt against the Macedonians and the system instituted by Philip. Arybbas and his family in their exile saw in this rebellion an opportunity to recover their kingdom, and accordingly their partisans in Epirus made a show of joining the confederates, while Aeacides, one of Arybbas' sons, married the daughter of Menon of Pharsalus, a leader of the revolt. But, of course, the exiles had no genuine interest in the Greek cause, and when Antipater, who was hard pressed, offered to acquiesce in their restoration if they abandoned their allies, the offer was accepted.[2] Even after the suppression of the rebellion

[1] Plutarch, *Alexander*, 68; Hypereides, *pro Euxenippo*, 36. Tarn, *C.A.H.* VI. 354, says that Olympias moved to Epirus in 331. This date is, perhaps, supported by Livy, VIII. 24, but I doubt whether she would have left Macedon before her brother's death.

[2] This reconstruction depends for the most part on the identification of the Aryptaeus of Diodorus, XVIII. 11, with King Arybbas. This identification was made in the first place by Reuss (*Rhein. Museum*, XXXVI. 161 seq.) and is accepted by Beloch (IV. 2. 146). The marriage of

Antipater continued to recognise Aeacides as king in Epirus, and it may be that he hoped that this would embarrass and weaken Olympias, who had been in sole control at Dodona for the last eight years and had given him constant trouble. In the event, however, the old queen established a complete ascendancy over Aeacides[1], and used him and his people for the furtherance of her own policy.

The one aim of this policy[2] was to maintain her son's empire intact for his heirs, his half-brother Philip Arrhid-aeus and his posthumous son by Queen Roxana. The joint succession of these two—the one an idiot, the other as yet unborn—had been recognised by the Macedonian army and its generals in Babylon, but Olympias far away in Dodona suspected, and was often right in suspecting, that the men who parcelled out Alexander's conquests among themselves were lacking in loyalty to the central authority and willing to convert their governorships into independent kingdoms. There was, of course, a series of regents of the Empire; first Perdiccas: then Antipater, who brought the two kings home to Macedon: then, on his death, Poly-perchon; but even in them Olympias had little faith and trusted rather to Eumenes of Cardia, who had been her son's chief secretary and was now striving against the separatist tendencies of Antigonus, Seleucus and the rest.

Aeacides with Menon's daughter Phthia (Plutarch, *Pyrrhus*, 1) is of itself proof that the exiled princes were mixed up in the Lamian War.

It is doubtful whether old Arybbas himself returned to Epirus, or whether the restoration was only effected in the person of Aeacides. Aeacides was preferred over his elder brother Alcetas (Justin, XVII. 3. 16; Pausanias, I. 11. 5) and Beloch contends that this preference cannot have been expressed either before 343 or during the exile, and that, therefore, Arybbas returned to reign for a short time after 322. On the other hand, Syncellus, p. 578 (see Appendix III), is not easily to be reconciled with a return of Arybbas to the throne.

[1] Pausanias, I. 11. 3.

[2] For the course of events from 323 to 301 see in general Beloch, IV. 1, chs. 3 and 4 (with references) and Tarn in *C.A.H.* VI. 15. In these notes I shall refer only to doubtful points.

He advised her to remain in Epirus until some order appeared out of chaos, but soon dissension in the royal family itself forced her to intervene. Eurydice, the wife of the idiot Philip, broke with Polyperchon, attached herself and her husband to Antipater's son Cassander, who had succeeded his father in the governorship of Macedon, and drove the regent, Queen Roxana and the little Alexander to take refuge in Epirus. Their cause was no concern of the Epirots, but Aeacides could refuse Olympias nothing, and in the autumn of 317 he invaded Macedon to restore them. The absence of Cassander and unwillingness of the Macedonians to fight against the mother of Alexander the Great combined to make the restoration easy. Eurydice and her husband were taken and killed; and Aeacides and his army went home. But when Cassander came north again from the Peloponnese, Olympias was hard pressed and called on Aeacides to help her again. A second campaign in the same year on behalf of a woman whom they detested was too much for the Epirots, and soon the discontent in the army became so great that Aeacides thought it wise to allow those who wished to return home. The result was disastrous, for a mere handful remained to face the enemy, while those who went home voted to depose their king and to make terms with Cassander.[1] Aeacides was helpless, and could do no better than take refuge in Aetolia, while in Epirus his friends were massacred and it was only by the devotion of a few attendants that his son Pyrrhus, a baby of two, was conveyed across the northern frontier to the court of the Illyrian chieftain, Glaucias.

Epirus was now once more connected with Macedon as

---

[1] The deposition of King Aeacides is described by Diodorus (XIX. 36. 4) as having been effected by a " Κοινὸν δόγμα τῶν Ἠπειρωτῶν ". This seems to refer to the delegate assembly of the "symmachy", but he can hardly have lost his Molossian crown without a popular vote of the Molossians also.

in the years from 330 to 322. There was no longer any king of the Molossians[1] and in place of Olympias, whom he had caused to be put to death, Cassander sent a certain Lyciscus to be "epimelete" or overseer of the country. The title of this official is characteristic of Cassander's policy with regard to the cities and countries which were dependent on him—not to interfere directly in their affairs, but to be represented on the spot by residents who would see to it that no decisions were taken against his interests. Such men were Demetrius of Phalerum at Athens, Damis at Megalopolis and Lyciscus in Epirus; and often, no doubt, they combined their duties as Cassander's resident with some office recognised in the local constitution.[2] There is, therefore, no doubt that in Epirus the various tribal assemblies, and even perhaps the inter-tribal assembly of delegates, continued to meet during this period, and it is possible that these bodies functioned with greater freedom than in the days when Olympias and Aeacides had ruled at Dodona: for the unpopularity of these two may have been as much due to an autocratic government at home as to their foreign policy. If this was so, the opposition between the friends and enemies of the Macedonian connection was not unlike an opposition between democrats and monarchists.

Meanwhile the theory of an undivided empire endured, and though Alexander's heir, the little son of Roxana, was no better than a prisoner in Cassander's castle at Amphipolis, the cause of unity was championed in his own interests by the ablest of all the "successors". By 315 Antigonus had crushed Eumenes, driven Seleucus to take

[1] It is commonly supposed that there was no break in the line of Molossian kings, but the natural deduction from Diodorus, xix. 36, is that Cassander set up a republic in 317. See for this question Appendix III, p. 106. In Appendix IV, p. 112, I have suggested that *S.G.D.I.* 1340 is to be placed in these years.

[2] For "epimeletes" see Tarn, *Antigonos Gonatas*, p. 196 n. 97, and Ferguson, *Hellenistic Athens*, p. 47 n. 3.

refuge in Egypt, and was in control of nearly every province from the Aegaean Sea to the Indian border. Only Ptolemy in Egypt, Lysimachus in Thrace, and Cassander with Macedon and a growing control over Greece, stood between him and universal empire. It was the last—Greece itself—that was the vital point; for the view which is sometimes expressed that in the hellenistic age the centre of gravity in the Mediterranean world shifted from Greece to the Levant is a misconception. It was the Greek element in each hellenistic monarchy which gave it its strength, and the control of the source, though its territory was small enough, was of greater value than many satrapies in Asia. To hinder such a control by Cassander Antigonus sent a succession of agents to Greece between 315 and 312 with money to stir up opposition to him. They were nowhere better received than by the Aetolians, who had never been subdued by Antipater or his son, and since it was among them that Aeacides the Molossian had taken refuge, it was not long before he had the support necessary for an effort to regain his throne. Even his defeat and death in battle near Oeniadae did not put an end to the attempt, for his brother Alcetas took his place as pretender, and kept Epirus in a state of turmoil until Cassander, with the same wisdom that his father had shown ten years before, offered to recognise him as king of the Molossians if he would become an ally of Macedon. The offer was accepted, and Alcetas' position was no doubt confirmed by the general peace between the "successors" in the following year.[1]

---

[1] Diodorus, XIX. 66. 74, 88–9; Pausanias, I. 11. 4–5. The reason why Aeacides was restored in 321 rather than his elder brother was probably that he was the son of Olympias' sister Troas, while Alcetas was a child of an earlier marriage. It is inherently quite probable that Arybbas' marriage with Troas about 359 was not his first, for his brother Neoptolemus cannot well have been born after 395 and the "consenuit" of Justin, VII. 6. 12, implies that he himself was born not much later. Alcetas II had sons grown up in 314. See Appendix III, p. 106.

It was a condition of this peace that the Greeks should be "free", but nevertheless within a few years the successors were all interfering once more with their liberties, and in 307 Antigonus made a great effort to win Greece for himself with a fleet and an army under the command of his son, the famous Prince Demetrius. Its arrival was a signal to the enemies of Cassander everywhere, and at the news of it in Epirus the nationalists murdered King Alcetas for his Macedonian sympathies. In his place they received back his nephew Pyrrhus from exile in Illyria—a boy of twelve who reigned for the next four years under a regency.[1] Demetrius naturally supported the young man's rule, but political considerations seem at first sight insufficient to explain his marriage with Pyrrhus' sister, which was celebrated in the Heraeum at Argos in 303; for the bridegroom was the heir to the greatest power in the world, while Deidameia's brother had nothing but the uncertain tenure of the kingship of a small tribe. But the match was not so unequal, for we must remember that the bride had a dowry of unique rank. Within the last few years the sons of Alexander the Great, his heir by Queen Roxana and his bastard by Barsine,[2] had both been murdered, and with them the direct male line of the royal house of Macedon, descended from Hercules, was extinguished. In recognition of this fact the "successors" had dropped all form of subordinate governorship and adopted the title of "kings", but as yet this "new monarchy" had no basis beyond the

[1] Diodorus, XIX. 89. 3, gives no date for the murder of Alcetas II and says that it was occasioned by his cruelty. Pausanius, I. 11. 5, mentions that Pyrrhus was restored as a consequence of it. Justin, XVII. 3. 21, and Plutarch, *Pyrrhus*, 3, show that this restoration took place in 307/6. I think that the account in the text is a reasonable combination of these statements.

[2] It is probable that Heracles, Alexander's supposed illegitimate son by Barsine, was not in fact his son at all—Tarn, *J.H.S.* 1921, p. 18 seq.—but it was generally believed that he was.

possession of material power. Deidameia, by contrast, was the descendant of Achilles and her ancestors had ruled in Molossia from immemorial antiquity. Olympias had destined her to be the wife of Roxana's son, and by marrying her Demetrius raised himself above the other "successors" to the level of Philip and Alexander.[1] It is significant that in the year after his marriage he revived Philip's pan-hellenic league, and thought to lead a united Greece against Cassander, the murderer of Philip's heirs and the usurper of his throne. But meanwhile in Asia his father Antigonus was faced with a coalition of his rivals who saw that now, if ever, his ambition for universal empire must be checked. Lysimachus crossed the Hellespont from Thrace; Seleucus, who had recovered his eastern satrapies, marched westwards, bringing with him a monstrous force of five hundred elephants, trained for war and bought from Chandragupta at the price of Alexander's Indian conquests; even the cautious Ptolemy moved up the coast of Palestine and invaded Syria. To meet the crisis Demetrius was recalled from Greece, and his withdrawal meant in many districts the revival of Cassander's power. It was so in Epirus, and within a few months Pyrrhus was following after his brother-in-law: but one may doubt whether he took the loss of his kingdom much to heart, for clearly a great battle was impending and he would be in at the death.[2]

[1] Cassander had married Philip's daughter Thessalonica (Diodorus, XIX. 52. I)—"σπεύδων οἰκεῖον αὐτὸν ἀποδεῖξαι τῆς βασιλικῆς συγγενείας"—but this was considered to have been a forced match. For the marriage of Demetrius and Deidameia, see Plutarch, *Dem.* 25.

[2] Pyrrhus' second exile—which is dated by Plutarch (*Pyrrhus*, 4) about 302—is clearly connected with Demetrius' withdrawal from Greece in the autumn of that year.

CHAPTER III

THE HELLENISTIC PRINCE

IN the last chapter I tried to show that the settlement reached at Corinth in 337 was a fulfilment of the current tendencies of Greek constitutional development and offered good hopes of an eventual union of Greece within herself and with Macedon. In the event, however, it proved a failure, and looking back, men saw in its author King Philip little but the destroyer of democratic liberty. The greatness of his son—a greatness that has not often been underestimated—and the unattractiveness of his own character have further combined to cast a shadow over him. He had none of the glory of a successful general, for though he made the Macedonian army, it was Parmenion, the officer of his choice, who led it to victory. In his conduct of affairs he was indefatigable, resourceful and unscrupulous, but no one has discovered in him that vision of genius which has been so freely claimed for his son. Nor did the man redeem the king. There were traditions of indulgence at the court of Pella and it may be that he did not overstep their bounds, but in the eyes of the Greeks his life was that of a drunkard and a debauchee. Yet with it all he was more than the Sulla of Greek history, for he entertained, even if he did not originate, constructive political ideas, and the title of greatness cannot be denied to one who combined such energy and such passions with a capacity to receive advice and a sense of proportion.

With Alexander it was very different.[1] After his defeat

---

[1] It is interesting to compare Beloch, IV. 2. 290 seq. with Tarn, *C.A.H.* VI, ch. 13, 431 seq. One is led by his dislike of "heroes" in history greatly to underestimate the personal qualities of Alexander, the other by his admiration of Alexander as a personality to minimise his defects as a statesman.

at Issus the king of Persia offered to give up all his territories west of the Euphrates—offered, in fact, the frontiers
which for six hundred years were to be the eastern bound
of the Roman Empire. All, and far more than all the conquests which Philip had contemplated were included in this
cession, and Parmenion, Philip's old general, is said to have
declared that if he were Alexander he would accept the
terms. The famous answer—"And so would I, if I were Parmenion"—may belong to legend, but the spirit of it is true
enough. Alexander was justly conscious that he was not as
other men, and nothing short of the complete conquest of
the Persian Empire would content him. Reasons of strategy
have been discovered to justify his desire, but reason enough
is that he knew that it was "passing brave to be a king and
ride in triumph through Persepolis"—and on he rode
through Babylon and Susa, through Ecbatana and Samar-
cand. At such a distance Greece seemed a little country
and her battles, "battles of mice".[1] The Greek contingents in the army, which were the visible sign that Alexander
was "hegemon" of a Greek confederacy, leading the forces
of hellenism on a crusade, were sent home when he determined to become the successor of Darius and to fuse East
and West in one universal dominion. One may admire the
grandeur of his conception and still more the strength of
personality which enabled him to flout every opposing
prejudice and to elevate orientals to posts of command,
but any chance that his dream might be realised was
destroyed by his early death, and meanwhile in the pursuit
of an ideal of world unity the possibility of a union of
Greece with Macedon vanished for ever.

We have seen that there were two factors in the settlement of 337—a confederacy of Greek cities and, standing
outside it and sustaining it, a "hegemon", the king of Mace-

[1] With reference to the battle of Megalopolis: Plutarch, *Agesilaus*,
15.

don. At the outset of the Persian expedition Alexander was true to the part assigned him. The spoils taken at the Granicus were dedicated by "Alexander *and the Greeks*" while the cities of Asia Minor liberated from Persian rule seem not to have been placed directly under Alexander's control, but to have become members of the confederacy. How completely his attitude had changed before his death is shown by the famous rescript issued from Babylon in 324 ordering the restoration of all exiles in Greece to their various cities. Even if the policy of that order was defensible, it is clear that such a restoration was a matter peculiarly within the competence of the council of delegates at Corinth and not properly to be settled from the outside by a "Command" of the "hegemon". In fact, however, Alexander no longer regarded himself as merely "hegemon", for coupled with this order regarding the exiles came a request that the Greek cities should pay him divine honours. There was, of course, nothing shocking to the Greek conscience in the deification of living persons, but in this case the deification created an entirely new and direct relation between each city and Alexander, the new god. The intermediate agency—the pan-hellenic organisation—was no longer required and was bound to die an early death. Thus both the factors which made for a union of Greece disappeared in face of the need to co-ordinate a world-empire of which Greece formed only a small part.

In the years which followed the death of Alexander the idea of a universal monarchy was gradually superseded by the growth of a number of separate kingdoms governed by various of his generals, but it needed half a century of constant warfare to settle how many such kingdoms there were going to be and who was going to rule in each of them. The history of this period of transition is apt to repel the modern reader, for it is complicated and—as it survives to us—little but the record of the conflicting ambitions of a group of warring princes. If more of the literature of the time had been preserved so that we could shift the emphasis a little from the chronicles of court and camp, it might prove a period of greater interest than that which went before it, for these years saw the reaction of the Greek world to the new situation created by the conquests of Alexander following hard upon the blow dealt by his father to the old order at home. In the "hellenistic" age many problems of politics and of personal ethics appeared in a fresh light, but here we need only take count of one development. We saw that in the fourth century philosophers had tended to look hopefully towards "enlightened monarchy" as a substitute for democratic licence. Alexander had raised a crop of monarchs and one may naturally ask whether the hellenistic king fulfilled these hopes or whether he was merely old tyrant writ large. To such a question there is no short answer. Monarchy never won many Greek hearts, but in most hellenistic kingdoms there were other elements which welcomed it. Some of the kings could claim to rule by no better title than that of the old-fashioned tyrant—the possession of men, money and fortresses—but others could point to the affection or the more or less sincere adoration of their subjects, while one at least accepted the theory that the monarch is the servant of his people.[1] It is impossible to fit the early hellenistic kings into any one category, but as things settled down there emerged from the most diverse elements—the tribal kingship, philosophic conceptions of enlightened rule, the majesty of oriental despots and Greek readiness to deify the powerful—a conception of monarchy which has had a long history in Europe.

[1] Antigonus Gonatas. For hellenistic monarchy in general see Kaerst, II. 296 seq.; *C.A.H.* VII. ch. I (Ferguson); Beloch, IV. 1. 364 seq.

In this chapter we shall be concerned with a representative of the first period—King Pyrrhus—who is by far the most famous figure in Epirot history and has even gained—on account of his war with the Roman republic—a certain general reputation denied to more notable contemporaries. His career is interesting as illustrating the utter confusion of affairs in the half-century which followed the death of Alexander the Great, and in our narrow field—the constitutional history of Epirus—his reign is very noteworthy, since in his hands the old Molossian kingship became a hellenistic monarchy extending not only over all Epirus, but far beyond its boundaries and including at one moment the Greeks of Italy and Sicily. In his capacity as king of the Molossians Pyrrhus occupied a position different from that of the other kings of his age, for he inherited limitations on his power, which were to some extent implied in the old tribal monarchy and had been extended and defined, as I have tried to show in the last two chapters, during the hellenisation of the country. To him these limitations were formal only, for he spent several of the most impressionable years of his life in attendance upon some of the most absolute of the "successors", and brought back with him from Ptolemy's court at Alexandria a conception of the place of the monarch in the state which was not at all in accordance with the traditional constitution of his people. His bravery, his great powers of generalship and the fame which his victories brought with them endeared him to his Epirot subjects and led them to acquiesce in his absolutism, but with the Greeks with whom he came in contact Pyrrhus was far less successful. Syracusans and Tarentines had no use for a warrior prince when once the victory was won, while Pyrrhus for his part was quite innocent of the culture and of the arts of accommodation and of management which alone could have made his monarchy tolerable to a Greek population. Even the Epirots—as his successors were to find to their cost—demanded their old liberties when the victories which had been their substitute for them ceased to be won.

We left Pyrrhus an exile from his kingdom on his way to join his brother-in-law Demetrius in Asia Minor on the eve of the final struggle between old Antigonus and his rivals. He was barely eighteen years old,[1] and the camp of the greatest of Alexander's successors was a very different place from his native Dodona, but from the first he was at home in the new atmosphere. Antigonus interested himself in him,[2] and Demetrius preferred him above his own son, the future King Antigonus Gonatas, a young man of about Pyrrhus' age, but studious and not at all a child after his father's heart.[3] Within a few months of his coming the defeat at Ipsos destroyed the Antigonid Empire in Asia, and Pyrrhus, who had fought at Demetrius' side in the battle, now accompanied him back to the Aegaean Sea and Greece. Their case was not desperate, for Demetrius' fleet based on the islands and a few coast towns kept him a power in the world, and the victors of Ipsos were quick to fall apart when once the dread of old Antigonus was gone.[4] From two of them, Cassander of Macedon and Lysimachus of Thrace, Demetrius had nothing but enmity to look for; but the others were prepared to be reconciled with him, and within two years he had formed an alliance with Seleucus, which was soon followed by a treaty with Ptolemy. It was one of the terms of this treaty that Pyrrhus, who had spent the last few years in charge of Demetrius' scanty possessions in Greece, should go to Ptolemy's court in Alexandria as a first step towards his

[1] For Pyrrhus' birth in 319–18 see Klotzsch, p. 95 n. 1.
[2] The Antigonus of Plutarch, *Pyrrhus*, 8, is, in my opinion, Monophthalmos, though Tarn (*Antigonos Gonatas*, p. 115 n.) suggests that it is Gonatas.
[3] For Gonatas' eclipse by Pyrrhus see Tarn, *ibid*. pp. 19–20.
[4] See in general Tarn in *C.A.H.* VII. 75–9 and Beloch, IV. 1. 214–16.

restoration to Epirus.[1] Such a restoration could hardly be effected against the will of Cassander, and while it was certain that the king of Macedon would oppose any "protégé" of Demetrius, there were circumstances which suggested that he might give his tacit consent to Pyrrhus' return under Ptolemy's aegis.

When the Macedonian party among the Molossians had driven out Pyrrhus they established as king in his place a certain Neoptolemus, who was probably a grandson of the late King Alcetas II.[2] In theory Epirus remained an independent country, but in fact Cassander once more exercised as complete a control over it as in the years between 317 and 312, and one of his first acts after the news of Ipsos freed him from any immediate fear from Demetrius had been to march a force across Neoptolemus' territory and to lay siege to Corcyra.[3] The island was at this time in the hands of Cleonymus, a prince of Sparta turned freebooter, and his piracies were, perhaps, the immediate excuse for the attack, but Corcyra had hampered Cassander's western policy in the past, and the possession of it would consolidate his control of Epirus.[4] There was, however, another

[1] When Tarn says (p. 77) that Pyrrhus at Alexandria "abandoned Demetrius and joined Ptolemy" he seems to me to be rather overstating the case. Pyrrhus' hostility to Demetrius dates from the latter's accession to the throne of Macedon (294): in 298 Demetrius may very well have desired his restoration to Epirus and have had it in mind when he sent Pyrrhus to Egypt. Proxenos' account (Plutarch, *Pyrrhus*, 4) represents the young hostage Pyrrhus as so captivating the court at Alexandria that Ptolemy determined to find him a throne and a wife: but this is not likely to have been the whole truth.

[2] For Neoptolemus see Appendix III, p. 106.

[3] Cassander and Corcyra: Diodorus, XIX. 78. 1 and XXI. 2.

[4] Cleonymus seized Corcyra in 303/2, Diodorus, XX. 104. Cary, *C.A.H.* VII. 634, follows Tillyard, *Agathocles*, p. 210, in saying that Demetrius occupied the island about 302. There is no evidence of any sort for this statement, for the fragment of Demochares to which Tillyard refers deals with the events of 291. Beloch (IV. 1. 203) thinks that Trogus, *Prologue* 15, shows that Cleonymus had lost Corcyra before Cassander's attack, but I doubt this deduction.

power interested in the Adriatic. Eighty years before, the tyrant Dionysius of Syracuse had desired Corcyra, and now the tyrant Agathocles, whose position and policy were in many ways the same as his predecessor's, sent his fleet to drive away Cassander's besieging force and to capture the island for himself.[1] Corcyra surrendered to her liberators, and this success encouraged the tyrant to imitate his predecessor once more, and to set a friendly prince on the throne of Molossia. He was an ally of Ptolemy,[2] and now joined him in pressing for Pyrrhus' restoration. In face of their insistence Cassander, who was dying of consumption, consented to a compromise by which the exile was to return, but was to share his crown with Neoptolemus, the friend of Macedon; and in the spring of 297 an Egyptian squadron escorted Pyrrhus and his queen, Ptolemy's stepdaughter Antigone, back to Epirus. Within a few months Cassander was dead[3] and before the end of the year his eldest son, Philip, was dead also, leaving the kingdom in the hands of his mother Thessalonica, as regent for his two younger brothers. Pyrrhus was quick to seize the occasion of this weakness in the government of Macedon to rid himself of his colleague on the throne. The official story spoke of a plot against his life frustrated by the timely execution of Neoptolemus, but Pyrrhus would not have shrunk from

[1] Agathocles and Corcyra: Diodorus, XXI. 2, and Plutarch, *Moralia*, 557 C.

[2] Agathocles' alliance with Ptolemy seems to be proved by his marriage with the Lagid Princess Theoxene. His children by her were "parvuli" in 290 (Justin, XXIII. 2. 6), but since he himself was born in 361 the marriage is not likely to be much after 300.

[3] Cassander seems to have died between April and June 297 (de Sanctis, *Riv. d. Fil.* N.S. VI. 1, on the strength of Pap. Ox. 2082), and if Dion Cassius (frg. 40) is right in saying that Pyrrhus negotiated with his son Philip who only reigned to be four months (Eusebius, I. 241; cf. Justin, XVI. 1. 1) it is obvious that the restoration must have taken place at the latest in the summer of the same year. I think myself that it probably took place in the spring, before Cassander's death, but the point cannot be proved.

an unprovoked murder to achieve the sole possession of his kingship[1]—a kingship which he held undisturbed for a quarter of a century.

From the moment of his accession two principles directed his policy. The history of his country during the last half-century taught the unmistakable lesson that a strong Epirus, and especially a strong monarchy in Epirus, was incompatible with a strong Macedon; therefore to conquer, or at the least permanently to weaken, the neighbouring kingdom was the constant object of his foreign policy. At home, meanwhile, he sought to change his Molossian kingship into an Epirot monarchy, and to strengthen it after the model of the hellenistic monarchies with which he had become acquainted in the most impressionable years of his life. He desired to be king of a united Epirus in as full a sense as Cassander or Demetrius were kings of Macedon. He came near to achieving both these objects, but in the end he achieved neither, and the cause of his failure was perhaps as much as anything an inability to strike a just balance between them. His feverish anxiety not to be dependent on Macedon led him into enterprises that cost time and energy which should have been devoted to the consolidation of his kingdom.[2]

Within the first few years of his reign he was given an opportunity to intervene with advantage in the affairs of Macedon.[3] There the regent, Queen Thessalonica, had planned to divide the kingdom between her two surviving

[1] Plutarch, *Pyrrhus*, 5, contains what seems to be the official version of Neoptolemus' death. It occurred during the lifetime of Queen Antigone, i.e. before 295 (Beloch, IV. 2. 148), but the exact date cannot be determined. It is clearly to be brought into connection with the weakness of Macedon after the death of Cassander.

[2] Wilamowitz, *Staat und Gesellschaft*, p. 154.

[3] For Pyrrhus' reign between 297 and 280 our chief authorities are Plutarch (*Pyrrhus*, 6–13, and *Demetrius*, 36–46) and Justin (bk XVI). There are modern accounts by Beloch, IV. 1, ch. 6; Tarn, *Antigonos*

sons; but the elder of them, Prince Antipater, dissatisfied with the arrangement, murdered his mother and sought to deprive his brother, Alexander, of his share of their inheritance. To oppose him Alexander appealed to Pyrrhus and offered him in return for his assistance the Macedonian border provinces of Tymphaea and Parauaea,[1] the city and district of Ambracia, and all the control and influence which he possessed in Acarnania[2] and Amphilochia. The offer was accepted, and on his side Pyrrhus invaded Macedon and brought Antipater to terms, but retired discreetly before the end of the year in time to avoid an embarrassing situation. Alexander had looked for help not only in Epirus but also from Demetrius,[3] who had by now returned from the Levant, and was engaged in recovering something of his old position in Greece. He marched northwards in answer to the appeal, but by the time of his arrival on the Macedonian frontier Alexander was no longer in need of his troops. It was a difficult situation, and in his attempts to induce his ally to go away quietly the young man gave Demetrius an opportunity of murdering him at a dinner-party and of having himself proclaimed in his place. The

Gonatas, chs. 2–5, and *C.A.H.* VII. ch. 3; and Klotzsch, pp. 153–218. In these notes I have not thought it necessary to give references to any but doubtful points.

[1] Which—as I have suggested, p. 38 above—was perhaps taken from Epirus by Philip in 352 or 343.

[2] It has been suggested that "Atintania" should be read for "Acarnania" in Plutarch, *Pyrrhus*, 6, as one of the provinces ceded to Pyrrhus by Alexander. Atintania appears to have been Macedonian in 314 (Diodorus, XIX. 67. 6) and clearly it could not have remained Macedonian after the cession of Parauaea. Probably, therefore, it was handed over at the same time. But Acarnania should be left in the text of Plutarch, for it hangs together with Amphilochia and Ambracia as an "ἐπίκτητον ἔθνος", whereas Atintania would probably be described as "τῆς Μακεδονίας" like Parauaea.

[3] The fact that Alexander appealed both to Pyrrhus and Demetrius should be noticed. Language is sometimes used which suggests that the two princes were enemies at this time. In fact they were perfectly good friends until Demetrius became king of Macedon.

new king followed up this success by driving Antipater
from his half of Macedon and thus gained all Cassander's
kingdom for himself. For the moment he recognised
Pyrrhus' possession of the districts which Alexander had
ceded to him and there was peace between them, but
clearly Demetrius, whose ambition equalled Pyrrhus' own,
was likely to prove a difficult neighbour.

The extent of Epirus was enormously increased by the
ceded provinces, and in these years there was yet another
accession to it in the form of the islands of Corcyra and
Leucas, the dowry of Lanassa, daughter of Agathocles of
Syracuse, whom Pyrrhus married after the death of his
Queen Antigone. But it was a heterogeneous kingdom
only held together by the person of its sovereign. The
original Epirot tribes—in particular the Molossians—remained the kernel of the whole, but Pyrrhus realised that
he must be more than a Molossian king if he was to make
a hellenistic state out of his various dominions. At Passaron,
no doubt, he paid a formal respect to the traditional limitations of the local kingship; the Epirot symmachy seems to
have endured throughout his reign,[1] and by its survival
implied that in Epirus sovereignty was not concentrated in
the person of the monarch; but much of Pyrrhus' power
now came from outside his old frontiers, and to emphasise
the change in his condition he transferred his residence
from Dodona to Ambracia. His new capital was con-
veniently situated on the coast in the middle of his do-

[1] The spoils taken from the Romans in the battle at Heraclea were
dedicated by "King Pyrrhus and the Epirots" (*S.G.D.I.* 1368). This
may be compared with the dedication of the Granicus' spoils by
"Alexander and the Greeks" and perhaps indicates that the Epirot
symmachy existed throughout Pyrrhus' reign. It is worth noticing
that Pyrrhus is always described as "the Epirot" whereas Alexander I
is nearly always "the Molossian". This probably means that the
Epirot tribes other than the Molossians recognised Pyrrhus as their
king and not just as the Molossian king who was "hegemon" of a
league to which they belonged.

minions and he did something to make it a modest imitation of the great hellenistic cities. But Ambracia had one great disadvantage. It was no royal foundation, but an old Greek city proud of its past and at heart resentful at the loss of its liberties. Pyrrhus and his house were never popular there, and when their opportunity came the Ambraciots displayed a spirit of independence more really dangerous to royalty than the mob-violence of Alexandria or Antioch.[1]

Meanwhile the danger from Demetrius was increasing. In addition to his Macedonian kingdom he had already a measure of control over Greece such as Cassander had never exercised, and Greece, it must be remembered, had still reserves of effective man-power far greater than those of any hellenistic monarchy. Pyrrhus felt that it would be folly to delay his intervention any longer, and in 291 he opened hostilities, which were to continue with hardly a break for five years, with a raid on Thessaly designed to divert Demetrius from his siege of Thebes. He was beaten off, and soon Demetrius was able to take a pleasant and satisfactory revenge. Queen Lanassa was unhappily married, for her husband from motives of policy exercised the royal prerogative of polygamy and had just brought Birkenna, a daughter of his northern neighbour the Illyrian king Bardylis, to be his second consort in the palace at Ambracia. In disgust his Syracusan queen returned to her dower cities and invited Demetrius to come and take her as his wife with Corcyra and Leucas as rewards. She was encouraged to this step by a change in her father's policy which coincided happily with the change in her own affections. Agathocles, it seems, had been unable to persuade Ptolemy to join with him in a design which he entertained for a new war against Carthage, and therefore decided to drop his Egyptian alliance in favour of one with

[1] Polybius, XXII. 11. 9; Livy, XXXVIII. 9; Strabo, VII. 325.

Demetrius, who was always prepared to fall in with a grandiose scheme. In consequence Lanassa's behaviour met with his approval, and at about the time that Demetrius sailed to Corcyra to take possession of his new wife and her dowry, Agathocles sent envoys to him to negotiate the terms of a formal alliance.[1]

The king of Macedon was now stronger than ever, and began to dream of a reversal of the verdict of Ipsos and a restoration of the Antigonid Empire in Asia. All that was worst in Alexander lived on in Demetrius. A grasping ambition was common to many of the "successors", but in none of them was it so unrestrained, so insensate as in him. Unfortunately, too, his resources were now not entirely inadequate to his designs, and the preparations which he set on foot were viewed with the greatest alarm by Lysimachus and by Ptolemy. But there remained one Greek people that had never been satisfactorily subdued by any king of Macedon, and Demetrius felt that he could not safely transfer a large part of his forces to Asia until he had reckoned with the Aetolians. The difficulty inherent in a campaign in a mountainous country with no central point, only to be reduced in a series of minor operations, was increased by the danger of an attack from Pyrrhus, who had naturally become a close ally of the only power in Greece besides his own still independent of Macedon. Demetrius, however, was a competent general. Invading

[1] Diodorus, XXI. 15. Queen Theoxene was sent back to Alexandria about 290 (Justin, XXIII. 2) clearly—as it seems to me—because of a change of alliances (cf. Stratonice's return from Pella to Antioch about 252, Tarn, *Antigonos Gonatas*, pp. 369–70). To say with Tillyard (*Agathocles*, p. 220) that the courtesy with which Theoxene was treated is against any breach between Syracuse and Alexandria is to misconceive the spirit of the personal relations of hellenistic princes with one another. To attribute the change of alliances to the projected campaign against Carthage is purely a conjecture, but I do not believe for a moment that Agathocles' alliance with Demetrius was forced on him by the action of Lanassa (Tillyard, *ubi supra*).

Aetolia from the north in the spring of 289 and scattering its people to their mountain refuges, he left his general Pantauchos with a force adequate to prevent their re-union and marched himself north-westwards to meet the Epirots before they could join their allies. But Pyrrhus—whether by luck or skill[1]—slipped past him and completely defeated Pantauchos while Demetrius was ineffectually ravaging the outlying parts of Epirus. It is probable that in this first proof of his generalship the young king enjoyed a handsome superiority of numbers, but the reputation of the army that he had defeated and his own brave conduct in the field sufficed to raise him high in the esteem of his own people and even to give him a certain popularity with the defeated Macedonians. Encouraged by his success and by the news that Demetrius had fallen ill, withdrawn his troops from Epirus and retired to Pella, Pyrrhus now attempted a raid on Macedon itself, but this was beaten off, and when Demetrius, with a prudent change of policy, offered a peace which included the restoration of Corcyra and Leucas, he was willing to accept it.[2]

The prospect of Demetrius set free to invade Asia raised a storm of protest from Lysimacheia and Alexandria. Pyrrhus was told that he was purchasing a momentary respite at the price of certain destruction in the future, that none of them would be secure while Demetrius was at large, and that if he violated the peace which he had just concluded Ptolemy and Lysimachus would join with him in an attack on the king of Macedon. There was an element of truth in these arguments, but it was too small to justify Pyrrhus in plunging into another war when there was such

---

[1] Plutarch (*Pyrrhus*, 7. 3) speaks of Pyrrhus and Demetrius "missing each other". But it was very much to Pyrrhus' advantage that they should miss.

[2] We do not know the terms of the treaty made in the autumn of 289, but in spite of Plutarch, *Pyrrhus*, 10. 4, I think it likely that it provided for the return of Corcyra.

a need for him to organise and consolidate his kingdom. Nevertheless he fell in with the scheme, and at first his perfidy brought him nothing but success. In 288 Lysimachus and he invaded Macedon simultaneously from east and west, drove Demetrius down into Greece and divided the land between them at the river Axius. Then in the next year Pyrrhus intervened in Greece itself, relieved Athens, which had revolted from Demetrius, from siege by him and made a peace with him which confirmed his possession of half Macedonia. Finally in 286, when Demetrius had transferred a large part of his now much diminished army to Asia, Pyrrhus broke faith again and took possession of Thessaly.

For a brief moment the Epirot king, with his dominions stretching from the Adriatic to the Axius and from Illyria to the Aetolian border, seemed the most powerful prince in the Balkan peninsula. This illusion endured as long as Demetrius and his dwindling army were at large in Asia Minor, but when at last the great quarry was run to earth and locked up for ever, Lysimachus turned to show Pyrrhus that in all his perfidy he had been the dupe of a man far abler than himself. If only he had secured the whole of Macedon his position would have been tolerable, but a division of the most famous kingdom in the world could not possibly last for long, and between the alien Epirot and Alexander's old general the people's choice was certain. When Lysimachus invaded the western half of the country Pyrrhus was quite unable to maintain himself there, and acknowledged his weakness by abandoning his new kingdom without risking a battle in its defence.[1] With Macedon went Thessaly, and Pyrrhus' frontiers were now once more what they had been before the wars with Demetrius; but in every other respect his position was far less favourable

[1] Pyrrhus abandoned his half of Macedon without a battle (Plutarch, *Pyrrhus*, 12).

than it had been in those earlier years. Then he had been faced by an unpopular king of Macedon, and had been supported in his hostility to him by the Aetolians, and by the kings of Thrace and Egypt. Now Lysimachus ruled both Thrace and Macedon, and yet retained the friendship of Ptolemy and the Aetolians.[1] Pyrrhus' only possible ally against him was Demetrius' son Antigonus,[2] who governed what little was left of his father's empire, but his power hardly stretched beyond the walls of Corinth and Demetrias, and in any case Pyrrhus' behaviour in the last few years had given him no cause to be active in his support. In 283 Lysimachus raided Epirus,[3] while its king was away on his northern frontier, and permitted his Thracians to loot the royal tombs at Dodona. It was only a demonstration, but it may have encouraged the Acarnanians to declare themselves independent once more and it filled Pyrrhus with a fear that a renewal of the Macedonian suzerainty over Epirus was imminent. Under the influence of that fear he tried "to call in a new world to redress the balance of the old"; and undertook his famous expedition to Italy and Sicily: but before we describe it we must first go back a little to explain the circumstances which made his intervention there possible.

Fifty years before, Pyrrhus' cousin, King Alexander the Molossian, had crossed the Adriatic to champion the cause of hellenism in Italy against the native barbarians. His expedition had ended in his defeat and death, but this final failure had been due to dissensions between the king and

[1] The Aetolians remained friendly to Pyrrhus throughout—he took Aetolian mercenaries to Italy (Dionysius Halicarnassus, xx. 1)—but there is no evidence that they were ever hostile to Lysimachus. No doubt if he had lasted they would have become his enemies.

[2] The treaty between Antigonus and Pyrrhus is to be dated about 285 (Tarn, *Antigonos Gonatas*, pp. 115–16).

[3] Pausanias, 1. 9. 9. Tarn has suggested (*op. cit.* p. 120) that this expedition led to the freeing of Acarnania, but see Appendix VIII, p. 128.

his original allies, the Tarentines, and the effect of his earlier victories over the barbarians in some measure survived it.[1] Further, the outbreak of the great war between Rome and the Samnites soon after this time tended naturally to divert both the Samnites and Rome's allies the Lucanians from pressing southwards. The smaller Greek cities along the toe of the peninsula still suffered from time to time from the attacks of the Bruttians, attacks from which the Tarentines, while claiming to be their protectors, did little or nothing to relieve them—but for Tarentum itself these years were a period of considerable prosperity.[2] In 304, however, the Samnite war came to an end, and the consequent renewal of attacks from the Lucanians—assisted in the background by the victorious Romans—placed Tarentum once more in need of foreign assistance. The natural source of help for the Greek cities would have been the tyrant Agathocles of Syracuse; but Tarentum was at this time ruled by an oligarchy that had been closely allied to the Syracusan aristocracy supplanted by the tyrant, and the government preferred to engage a mercenary force under the command of the Spartan prince Cleonymus. The prince, however, was not markedly successful against the barbarians, and seems to have shown all the unfortunate personal qualities associated with "the Spartan abroad". Soon he retired to the island of Corcyra —which he had seized for his own use—and during his absence popular discontent with this champion of the oligarchs brought the democratic party into power in Tarentum.[3]

[1] For the circumstances in which Alexander came to make his Italian expedition see p. 40 above. For the course of the war and its results, Beloch, III. 1. 591, and C.A.H. VI. 300–301.

[2] Strabo, VI. 280. Diodorus, XIX. 3, describes how the Syracusans intervened in Italy to protect Croton from the Bruttians.

[3] Diodorus, XX. 104–5. The Tarentine government was certainly aristocratic in 314, for in that year it sent help to the Syracusan

This change opened the way for Agathocles to intervene in Italy. We have seen already how he rescued Corcyra from Cassander and kept it for himself. In Italy he pursued the same policy.[1] The Romans and other barbarians were kept off, and hellenism was preserved at the price of subservience to the tyrant. But his death in 289 was a fatal blow, for he left no successor to his power. In Sicily his empire broke up and the Carthaginians began gradually to threaten the Greek cities, while in Italy the usual Lucanian attacks began again at once. This time, however, the smaller Greek cities found a new way of answering them. Instead of appealing to the Tarentines, who had never as yet been of any use to them, or seeking the help of some other Greek power in Sicily or the motherland, they asked to be taken under the protection of Rome herself.[2] This request put the Romans in rather a difficult position, for the Lucanians were more or less their allies and in any case lower Italy had been hitherto outside the range of their policy. Eventually, however, after a few years of hesitation the "Expansionist" party in the senate prevailed. Thurii was taken under Rome's protection and on the refusal of the Lucanians to stop their attacks, the consul Fabricius drove them away and put a garrison in the town. Locri and Rhegion

oligarchs in their struggle against Agathocles: Diodorus, xix. 70. 8. At the same time it is clear that it was a democracy that called in Pyrrhus: p. 68 n. 1 below. When did the change occur? I think that the Italian activities of Agathocles in the 'nineties show that it is to be placed about 300 and I suggest that it is actually referred to in Diodorus (xx. 105. 1) when Cleonymus is said to have attacked Tarentum "to punish it for having revolted from him". It is characteristic of the difference between Agathocles and Dionysius that the one maintained his influence over Tarentum with the aid of demagogues and the other by means of the philosopher-courtier Archytas.

[1] For Agathocles and Corcyra see p. 57 above. For his activities in Italy: Beloch, iv. 1. 202 seq.

[2] A good account of Rome's intervention in Southern Italy between 290 and 280 is given by Beloch, *Römische Geschichte*, p. 460.

at once applied for garrisons too, and were occupied by Roman troops in the same year.

In Tarentum, meanwhile, opinion was sharply divided over these events. To the oligarchs, who had revived a little in influence since Agathocles' death, Thurii's action seemed very reasonable and one which they might be well advised to imitate. To the ruling democracy, on the other hand, it appeared as a betrayal of hellenism and an insult to their city.[1] Of recent years the Tarentine government had cultivated the friendship of King Pyrrhus the Epirot, and had lent him the aid of its fleet to regain possession of Corcyra:[2] now it began to look to him to intervene in the affairs of Italy and to check the advance of Rome. The oligarchs of the opposition, for their part, made a bold attempt to forestall him and to hand over their city to the Romans. It was arranged by them that the small Roman squadron lying at Thurii should appear in the harbour of Tarentum on the day of the great Dionysiac festival, when the attention of the bulk of the populace would be engaged in the theatre, and that under cover of its presence the pro-Roman party should force itself into power. Strictly speaking, the Roman warships had no right even to be at Thurii, for many years before, at the time of King Alexander's campaign, when South Italy was still quite outside

---

[1] That of the two parties at Tarentum the oligarchs wished to imitate Thurii and the democrats looked to Pyrrhus is clear from the account preserved in Dio, frg. 40 (cf. Zonaras, VIII. 2). This account derives from an aristocratic source—possibly the Aristarchus of Zonaras, VIII. 2. 15—and probably passed via Timaeus to Fabius Pictor and so into Roman history. It is, of course, very prejudiced against the leaders of the democracy—they are drunkards and worse.

[2] For Tarentum's help in the recapture of Corcyra: Pausanias, I. 12. 2. The date may be any time after Demetrius' departure to Asia (i.e. from 286 onwards) but if Justin (xxv. 4. 8) is right in saying that Ptolemaeus, Pyrrhus' son by Antigone, distinguished himself in the fighting, it can hardly be earlier than 281, for Ptolemaeus cannot have been born before 297. For Leucas see Appendix VIII, p. 132.

Rome's sphere of influence, the senate had bound itself by treaty not to send its warships beyond the Lacinian headland; but circumstances were now very different and the treaty might plausibly be held to have been abrogated. Unfortunately, however, the oligarchs had quite misjudged the temper of the people. The leading democrats denounced this flagrant attack on the city's liberty, and under the influence of their harangues the Tarentines streamed out of the theatre, manned a part of their ships and succeeded, after a sharp struggle, in sinking five of the Roman squadron, capturing another and putting the rest to flight. This success they followed up by marching on Thurii, expelling its pro-Roman government and forcing the Roman garrison to leave the town. Only the humblest submission would now be likely to avert war, and war could hardly be contemplated if Pyrrhus refused his assistance. Clearly, if he chose to cross to Italy he could make his own conditions.[1]

We have seen already how the faults of his policy in Greece had by this time placed King Pyrrhus in an embarrassing position. The great power of Lysimachus threatened to overwhelm him, and yet he had no allies on whose support he could rely. It was tempting to think of acquiring a kingdom in the West which would compensate him for the loss of Macedon. Greek Italy, it is true, did not promise much; but beyond Italy was Sicily, and Alexander, his son by Lanassa, was Agathocles' heir. He might hope to revive the tyrant's empire—indeed the confusion

---

[1] Appian, *Samnitica*, 7, also Dionysius, XIX. 4, Dio, XXXIX. 5, and Zonaras, VIII. 2. 1–2. Tenney Frank, in *C.A.H.* VII. 641, is not afraid of Beloch (IV. 1. 546) and follows Appian in saying that the Romans were the injured party and were only "having a look round"; I have no doubt that he is wrong. For the part played by the theatre cf. Thucydides, III. 3, and Plutarch, *Timoleon*, 10. The "old treaty" may have been made between the senate and Cleonymus, but the situation at the time of Alexander the Molossian's expedition seems more in harmony with its terms.

into which Sicilian affairs had fallen since Agathocles'
death seemed to call for such a revival. On the other hand,
there was much to be said against undertaking such an
expedition at this moment, and the king's chief adviser,
the Thessalian Cineas, was strongly opposed to it.[1] His
master—he could urge—would be wrong to regard his
present embarrassment as foreshadowing a condition of
permanent weakness, for the flux in politics which had set
in on the death of Alexander the Great was not yet abated.
Lysimachus was on the brink of war with Seleucus—a war
which might change the whole situation—and if Pyrrhus
engaged in a venture in the West he might not be able to
make use of his opportunities in Greece. It was better to
wait and see what happened.[2] Such considerations made
Pyrrhus hesitate to accept the invitation to intervene in
Italy, and his hesitation was at once reflected in the course
of events at Tarentum. An embassy had come from Rome
after the recent outburst[3] to demand the return of the
prisoners, the restoration of the pro-Roman government
to Thurii, and the surrender of the actual leaders of the
attack on the ships. These were not extravagant demands,
but the Tarentines—confident that Pyrrhus would soon be
at their side—had refused to comply with them. The senate
of necessity declared war, and, now when the consul
Aemilius and his legions had already invaded Tarentine
territory, it began to look as if Pyrrhus would not come
after all. In these circumstances the peace party gained

[1] In Plutarch, *Pyrrhus*, 14, Cineas is represented as opposing the
expedition to Italy. If he did so, the arguments which he used may not
have been unlike those which I have suggested for him.

[2] Justin, XVIII. 1. 1, mentions two embassies of the Tarentines to
Pyrrhus. It is natural to suppose that it was his hesitation which led to
the fluctuations in Tarentine politics described in Dio and Zonaras.

[3] For the famous Roman embassy to Tarentum—Postumius and
his gown, etc.—see Beloch's note on IV. 1. 546. The Romans were not
anxious for war and restricted their demands to a minimum: Appian,
Samnitica, 7.

very much in strength; a partisan of Rome was elected to the chief magistracy, and it was clear that it was now or never for Pyrrhus.

The news that Lysimachus had been defeated and killed in the battle of Corupedion must already have reached Ambracia,[1] but in spite of it Pyrrhus determined not to lose the chance of an empire in the West and sent Cineas with a small force to take possession of Tarentum, promising to follow himself in the next spring. It was the most important decision of his life and it proved disastrous, but it cannot be said that at the time of its making it was obviously wrong. The truth is that in these years important events followed quickly one upon another and were absolutely incalculable. Thus in the few months which separated the dispatch of the advance force and the crossing of the main army, the whole situation in Greece had once more changed completely. Seleucus—the last of the successors— who by his defeat of Lysimachus had united Macedon to his empire in Asia and for a brief moment ruled from Epirus to India, was murdered in February 280. The assassin—Ptolemy Keraunos—seized the throne of Macedon, but at least three princes—Seleucus' son Antiochus, Demetrius' son Antigonus and Pyrrhus himself—could all maintain that they had a better right to it than he. The Epirot may well have wished that he had not committed himself in Italy, but for the moment he could do no better with his claim than borrow a force of war-elephants and some thousands of Macedonian infantry from Keraunos as a price for abandoning it. With them, a force of mercenaries and his own Epirots—some twenty-five thousand men in all[2]—he crossed to Tarentum in the early spring. The need of him had been so great that the Tarentines

---

[1] It seems fairly clear that Corupedion was fought in the spring of 281: Beloch, IV. 2. 107 seq.

[2] Dionysius, xx. 1, and Tarn, *Antigonos Gonatas*, p. 426.

had placed themselves almost unreservedly in his hands, only exacting a promise that he would not remain in Italy longer than was necessary. It was, of course, well known that Sicily was his real object, but it was natural to fear that he would not readily withdraw his garrison from the citadel of Tarentum.[1]

The Romans were not well prepared to undertake a serious war in South Italy, for disturbances and revolts in Etruria called for the presence of the consul Coruncanius and his army in the north. But the other consul, Laevinus, was sent southwards through Lucania to the gulf of Tarentum, while Aemilius—a consul of the previous year—was ordered to remain at his post in Apulia. Pyrrhus had taken up a position on the river Siris near Heraclea and Laevinus had the confidence to attack him there. The numbers on each side were about equal, but Pyrrhus was by far the better general and one need not doubt that the Romans were disconcerted by their first encounter with elephants. Laevinus lost nine thousand men—killed or prisoners— abandoned his camp and fled with the remnants of his army to join Aemilius at Venusia.[2] An immediate result of the battle was that the citizens of Locri took their Roman garrison prisoners and went over to Pyrrhus.[3] Rhegion, too, would have done the same but for the energetic action of the commanding officer, Decius, who executed the most prominent citizens and held the town for Rome.[4] Pyrrhus

[1] The terms on which he came included the surrender of the citadel of Tarentum for the duration of the war. Pyrrhus had profited by the experience of Alexander the Molossian, who had been helpless in face of the ingratitude of his chief allies.

[2] A good account of the battle of Heraclea is given by Judeich in *Klio* (1926). Hieronymus (Plutarch, *Pyrrhus*, 17) puts the Roman losses at 7000 and Pyrrhus' at about 4000. Orosius, IV. 1. 11 (derived from Livy) says that 2000 prisoners were taken: Eutropius, II. 11, gives 1800. These are reasonable figures if one considers that Laevinus lost his camp.   [3] Justin, XVIII. 1. 9.

[4] Dio, frg. 40, 7–8; Appian, *Samnitica*, 9. See also p. 76 n. 2 below.

left him alone for the moment, for it was important to push forward quickly and win over the Lucanians and Samnites to his alliance. Encouraged by his reception among them, he decided to try the effect of a march northwards through Campania and Latium; but there he was disappointed. Capua and even the Greek Naples shut their gates against him, and though he plundered the Liris valley and advanced as far as Anagnia, he could not persuade the Latins to desert Rome. A siege of the city was out of the question, for Laevinus and Aemilius were following in his rear, and the legions recalled from Etruria blocked his further advance; so the army retired to winter quarters in Campania while Pyrrhus himself returned to Tarentum.[1]

About November a Roman embassy appeared, ostensibly in order to negotiate for the return of the prisoners taken in the battle. This was clearly an opportunity for discussing peace terms, and Pyrrhus, who had no wish to engage in a prolonged war in Italy, made the conclusion of a peace an indispensable condition of any arrangement touching his prisoners. Fabricius, the leader of the embassy, did not reject the idea, and a treaty was framed by which the Romans were to evacuate South Italy and acknowledge the independence of the Lucanians and Samnites, while Pyrrhus, on his side, would release all his prisoners free of ransom. Cineas, the king's minister, accompanied Fabricius back to Rome to obtain the ratification of the peace from the senate, and with him came a certain number of prisoners on "parole" to celebrate the Saturnalia and work on the feelings of the populace. On his arrival he set about visiting the most influential senators and attempted to distribute presents among them after the lavish fashion of hellenistic diplomacy. The Romans, however, in their simplicity were unable to distinguish presents from bribes

[1] For the negotiations between Pyrrhus and the Senate in 280/78 see Appendix V.

and received him coldly, nor was the peace party in the senate strong enough to gain a majority against the influence and oratory of Appius Claudius. The terms were, in fact, much harder than the military situation justified Pyrrhus in fixing, though they were the easiest that his alliance with the Samnites permitted him to offer. They were rejected, and Cineas returned with his prisoners to Tarentum.

Pyrrhus was now committed to another campaign. The march on Rome of the previous year had shown him that no sudden break-up of the Roman power was to be expected and that he must go to work gradually. Accordingly he planned to employ the campaigning season of 279 in reducing the various Roman strongholds in Apulia—chief among them the recently founded Latin colony of Venusia. The senate decided to risk a battle in its defence, and, since Pyrrhus' forces had now been considerably increased by contingents of Samnites and Lucanians both consular armies were concentrated to oppose him. The battle[1]— fought on the Aufidus, not far from Asculum—ended in a Roman defeat, and though it was by no means so decisive as that of Heraclea, it seems to have led to the consuls evacuating Apulia. But meanwhile news had reached Pyrrhus from Greece and Sicily which made him even more anxious than before to conclude an early peace with the Romans.

Since his murder of Seleucus, Ptolemy Keraunos had been fully occupied in defending the possession of his crown against claimants to it with better titles than his own, and had neglected the chief duty of a king of Macedon— the defence of his frontiers against the barbarians of the north. This neglect unfortunately coincided with a south-ward migration of the Celts from the regions of the Danube and the Save,[2] and in the spring of 279 hordes of this people

---

[1] Beloch, IV. 2. 275.
[2] de Navarro in *C.A.H.* VII. 65.

came down on Macedonia. Keraunos himself was killed in battle against them, his kingdom was overrun and the barbarians pressed on to the invasion of Greece.[1] Epirus lay off their path and was itself in no great danger, but clearly if Pyrrhus were in his own kingdom he would have an excellent opportunity both of regaining the crown of Macedon and of gaining a reputation as the saviour of Greece by a defeat of the barbarians. But, great though the temptation to return may have been, the inducement to go on to Sicily was greater. There, since Agathocles' death, petty tyrants had seized power in a number of the Greek cities, and meanwhile the Carthaginians were advancing gradually towards a control of the whole island.[2] Earlier in this year Hicetas of Syracuse had been defeated by them and had in consequence been supplanted in power by a certain Thoenon. Now Thoenon, in his turn, was besieged in the citadel of Syracuse by Sosistratus of Acragas, who was in possession of the city itself, while the Carthaginians prepared to take advantage of these dissensions to complete the ruin of hellenism in the island. It was clear that next year both Thoenon and Sosistratus would be besieged in Syracuse, and now both of them, without apparently sinking their differences, sent envoys to Tarentum to beg Pyrrhus to come to their assistance. This was just such an opening as Pyrrhus had desired, and the invaluable Cineas returned with the ambassadors to prepare the way for his master's intervention; while the king himself tried to conclude a peace with Rome which would satisfy his Italian allies.

The prospects of such a peace seemed hopeful, for the Romans had elected Fabricius, who was known to be opposed to a continuance of the war, to the consulship for 278 and when he appeared to take over the command of the

[1] Tarn, *C.A.H.* VII. 101 seq.
[2] Beloch, IV. 1. 541–4.

legions in Campania negotiations were at once set on foot. But it was in the interest of Carthage that Pyrrhus should be detained in Italy, and with this object in view the admiral Mago, with a fleet of a hundred and twenty warships destined for the blockade of the great harbour of Syracuse, appeared off Ostia in the spring of this year. His first move was to remind the senate of the alliance which subsisted between Rome and Carthage, and to tell it that his government was anxious to help the Romans in their difficulties by joining in an offensive against Pyrrhus. The senate replied that Rome required no assistance—that is to say, that it did not wish to compromise the negotiations—and Mago then sailed down the coast to visit Pyrrhus. We do not know the terms of their conversation, but we may guess that Pyrrhus was told that if he agreed not to go to Sicily Carthage would see to it that Rome agreed to a peace which would allow him to return to Greece, but that if he persisted in his Sicilian venture she would wreck the negotiations. The king, however, was not to be put off from his design of recreating Agathocles' empire, and Mago returned to Rome. This time he was more successful, for now that the senate knew that Pyrrhus was determined to leave Italy, it consented, in return for a large sum of money, to promise the Carthaginians never to make a separate peace with him.[1] Mago then set sail for Syracuse, taking on board with him five hundred Roman soldiers to strengthen the garrison of Rhegion that had been cut off from its base for nearly two years.[2] Pyrrhus, meanwhile, retired to Tarentum disappointed in his hopes of a peace, but set upon his Sicilian expedition.

[1] Beloch, IV. 2. 476, has reconstructed the treaty between Rome and Carthage, and Mattingly (*Numismatic Chronicle*, 1924, p. 181) has shown that Carthage had to pay for it.

[2] An excellent paper of Beloch's ("Die Campaner in Rhegion", *Klio*, I. 284) shows conclusively that Decius and his companions at Rhegion (p. 72 n. 4) were at this time still approved of by the Senate,

Half of what remained to him of the troops which he had brought from Greece the king left in Italy to defend his allies. With the rest—about ten thousand men[1]—he sailed from Tarentum in the autumn of 278. As a convoy he had only the Tarentine navy of some sixty ships, against which Mago could bring at least one hundred and twenty: but the Carthaginian admiral was unequal to his double task of blockading the harbour of Syracuse and of preventing Pyrrhus from crossing to Sicily.[2] At first he had left twenty ships at Messina and gone on with a hundred to Syracuse: later when he heard that the Greek fleet was under way he sent thirty more northwards. Even with this reinforcement, however, the squadron at the straits made no attempt to attack Pyrrhus, but allowed him to land at Taormina, and march southwards towards Syracuse while his fleet followed him along the coast. Mago, of course, had still as many ships at his command as Pyrrhus, and the Carthaginian army was no doubt far superior in numbers to the Greek, but nevertheless its generals raised the siege at the approach of the relieving force. They had a certain danger to fear from a sortie of the Syracusans either by land or sea, but it was probably Pyrrhus' reputation which influenced them most in their decision not to risk a battle.

and that the troops which Mago took on board were reinforcements for them. In spite of this, Frank, in *C.A.H.* VII. 650, says that they were "sent to surprise the mutinous garrison".

[1] The number of troops taken by Pyrrhus to Sicily was given in Appian, *Samnitica*, 11. The passage is corrupt, but a plausible emendation gives 8000 foot and 1000 horse.

[2] Diodorus, XXII. 8, says that Pyrrhus brought about sixty ships with him and found 140 at Syracuse. Mago appeared at Ostia with 120 ships (Justin, XVIII. 2), but since Diodorus (*ubi supra*) says that he blockaded Syracuse with 100 I have assumed that he left 20 at the Straits of Messina. The 30 others that he is said to have sent off "διὰ τινὰς χρείας ἀναγκαίας" must, I think, have been reinforcements for this squadron.

How great was that reputation was shown in a striking manner by his reception by the Sicilian Greeks. Men felt that here was not only a great general but a real "king", a man who had moved as an equal among the "successors" and was invested with something of the magic of Alexander. Domestic quarrels came to an end in his presence and the petty tyrants, who would not recognise each other's sovereignty, united in acknowledging his. Pyrrhus was acclaimed as "hegemon and king" of the Siceliots[1] with Lanassa's son Alexander as heir to his throne, and the various cities sent him contingents for the campaign against the Carthaginians which he opened in the next year.[2] This enthusiasm—combined with Pyrrhus' powers of generalship—sufficed to drive the enemy within six months behind the walls of the fortress of Lilybaeum in the west of the island, and so to cow them that they offered, if they were allowed to retain this last stronghold, to abandon their claim to all their other possessions in Sicily and to pay a war indemnity.[3] The king himself is said to have been willing to make peace on these conditions, but his allies persuaded him that it would be unwise to leave the Carthaginians with any base in Sicily, and urged him to capture Lilybaeum. In fact, however, the place was practically impregnable from the land side and Carthage still controlled the sea. After two months of a violent and expensive assault Pyrrhus realised that he must give up the attempt until he could fit out an adequate fleet. In the last year of his life Agathocles had been preparing an expedition

[1] Polybius, VII. 4. 5.

[2] Plutarch, *Pyrrhus*, 22, says that the king was in command of 30,000 infantry and 2500 horse in Sicily. If we were right in putting the force which he brought with him at about 9000, the Siceliots must have contributed more than 20,000. This does not seem an unreasonable figure. Sosistratus is said to have offered 10,000 and the tyrant of Leontinoi 4000.

[3] Plutarch, *Pyrrhus*, 23, and Diodorus, XXII. 10. 6. The latter represents the king as being willing to accept the terms.

to Africa and his armada still lay in the harbour of Syracuse, but the ships were in great need of repair after ten years disuse, and moreover there was a great shortage of men to sail them.

At Syracuse in the winter of 277 to 276 Pyrrhus considered his position. To understand his difficulties and the policy by which he sought to overcome them one must regard what had been happening in Greece since the Celtic invasion.[1] After Keraunos' death Macedon had been for some months in a state of utter confusion with the Gauls ravaging the countryside and the population in refuge behind the walls of the cities, but at length the crisis produced a man, and Sosthenes, while refusing the title of king, governed the country and restored some measure of order. Meanwhile those of the Gauls who had invaded Greece itself had been driven out again, and the Aetolians, to whom their defeat was chiefly due, had earned the title of saviours of their country. During these same years Seleucus' son Antiochus and Demetrius' son Antigonus—both of whom, it may be remembered, had claims to the crown of Macedon—had been waging an obscure war together. The chief seat of their operations seems to have been the regions about the Hellespont, but Antiochus naturally looked for allies among those of the Greeks who felt themselves threatened in their liberties by the remnants of the Antigonid dominion in Greece, and at this time the Spartans—under Cleonymus, who had by now returned to his native land—headed a coalition of Peloponnesian states in hostilities against Craterus whom Antigonus had left as his governor in Corinth. Then—sometime in the

[1] The scattered references on which the history of the years 280 to 277 in Greece rests are given and fitted together by Beloch, IV. 1. 559–68. I would add to them Plutarch, *Laconica, Archidamus*, 9 (Archidamus, son of Eudamidas), which seems to me to give what we have nowhere else—a reference to the conclusion of peace between Craterus (that is, Antigonus) and the Peloponnesian cities about 277.

course of 278—reason prevailed in the counsels of princes
for the first time for many years, and the two kings signed
a treaty of peace by which Antigonus renounced all his
interest in Asia—in the empire that his grandfather had
held and his father had always dreamed of regaining—
while Antiochus abandoned his claim to Macedon. At the
moment, indeed, the importance of this peace cannot have
been realised, for Antigonus was not yet in possession of
Macedon, but in the next year a victory which he won at
Lysimacheia over a horde of marauding Gauls recom-
mended him to the Macedonians and, since Sosthenes was
now dead, they received him as king. Meanwhile Craterus
had succeeded in ending the war with the Peloponnesian
states. A controlling influence was all that Antigonus
desired to exercise in Greece and therefore none of the
states became subject to him, but all of them were required
to enter into agreements not to tolerate an anti-Macedonian
policy. Even the Spartans abandoned the contest and
agreed to the exile of Cleonymus[1]—the chief enemy of
Antigonus in their city. Thus by 276 Antigonus was in
peaceful possession of most of what his father had held a
dozen years before, but his possession was by no means
firmly established. He had not yet won the affection of his
Macedonian subjects, for he was the son of a king whom
they had detested, and it was always possible that Pyrrhus,
who had driven Demetrius from his kingdom, would
return from the West and drive his son from it also.
Whether in fact Pyrrhus would abandon his claim to
Macedon or try to reassert it would depend on the view
which he took of his position in Italy and Sicily.

With that position—it might be urged—he had every
right to be contented. In Sicily he was in possession of

[1] Plutarch, *Pyrrhus*, 26, suggests that domestic difficulties were the
ground of Cleonymus' exile from Sparta—I have no doubt that his
hostility to Macedon was the chief cause.

a kingdom as extensive as that of Agathocles; in Italy he had a far surer control of the Greek cities than had either Agathocles or Dionysius before him; and in addition there was his own Epirus. Surely it would be a folly to risk the loss of all that he had gained in the West in a fresh attempt on the throne of Macedon? But there was another side to the picture. To begin with, Pyrrhus was no longer as popular in Sicily as he had been on his arrival there.[1] In electing him "king and hegemon" the Siceliots had followed the model of the league of Corinth, that is to say they intended their king to stand to them much as Philip had stood to the Greeks, but Pyrrhus chose to behave as though they had placed themselves as unreservedly in his hands as had the Tarentines. The result was discontent issuing in conspiracy against him, and in this very winter Thoenon was executed for treason, while Sosistratus took refuge with the Carthaginians. Then, too, it was becoming plain that there would be no following up of his victories over the Carthaginians in Sicily with an invasion of Africa, for it was impossible to raise an adequate fleet.[2] A severe and most unpopular conscription of oarsmen sufficed to man only a third of Agathocles' warships. Finally his allies among the Italians were clamouring for his return. The garrisons which he had left behind were amply sufficient to protect the Greek cities of the coast,[3] but the Lucanians and Samnites in the interior could not preserve their independence against the Romans without his assistance.[4]

---

[1] Plutarch, *Pyrrhus*, 23.

[2] Diodorus, XXII. 8, speaks of him as having 200 ships, i.e. about 60 which he brought from Tarentum and about 140 that he found at Syracuse; but since he had only 110 in the sea-fight in 276 (Appian, *Samnitica*, 12) it seems probable that he could equip and man only about 50 of Agathocles' vessels.

[3] Appendix V (III).

[4] Zonaras, VIII. 6; Plutarch, *Pyrrhus*, 23; Justin, XXIII. 3. 5.

It is not probable that Pyrrhus at this time definitely decided to return to Greece, but such considerations as I have outlined led him to think there was more need and use for his presence in Italy than in Sicily, and in Italy, incidentally, he would be in a better position to intervene in Greek affairs if he desired to do so. Accordingly in the autumn of 276 the Epirot army was shipped back from Syracuse to Locri; but its withdrawal did not at all imply that Pyrrhus had abdicated his Sicilian kingship. If we may trust the sole authority of Justin[1] he had, before withdrawing, inflicted yet another defeat on the Carthaginians, and he seems to have left his son Alexander behind him to represent his interests in the island.[2] On landing in Italy he proceeded at once to the siege of Rhegion, a city, it may be remembered, then held for Rome by a force of Campanian mercenaries that had enslaved the Greek population. To relieve the place by land was beyond the powers of the Roman senate, but in pursuance of the treaty of alliance of 278 the Carthaginians sent their fleet into the Straits of Messina to break the blockade, and in the sea-fight which followed seventy

[1] Justin, XXIII. 3. 9.
[2] Justin (XVIII. 2. 12) says that Alexander was left at Locri when his father crossed to Sicily, but since later he clearly confuses him with his brother Helenus (XXIII. 3. 3), it seems probable that it was Helenus who was left at Locri while Alexander was taken to Sicily. This would have been the natural course, for Lanassa's son was to be the future king of the island. Further, it seems to me probable that he remained at Syracuse when Pyrrhus returned to Italy. Helenus, who was left at Tarentum on his father's return to Greece, was recalled for the Peloponnesian expedition of 272 (Justin, XXV. 3. 4, and Plutarch, *Pyrrhus*, 34) in which Ptolemaeus, Pyrrhus' eldest son and the heir to the Epirot throne also took part. Of Alexander, on the other hand, we hear nothing until we find him king of Epirus in 271. If he had been in Greece from 275 to 272 he must have been left behind as governor in Epirus during the campaign in the Peloponnese, but he is more likely to have stayed at Syracuse until the news of the disastrous issue of that campaign reached him. This residence of his at Syracuse from 275 to 272 would explain his close relations with Hieron after his accession.

out of a hundred and five Greek warships were sunk.[1] The siege of Rhegion had, of course, to be abandoned, and Pyrrhus withdrew his army to winter in Tarentum, but the consequences of the defeat were more far-reaching than this. By it the fleets of Tarentum and Syracuse—the only naval powers among the Greeks of the West—were crippled, and the naval supremacy of the Carthaginians assured. In these circumstances it was hopeless to think any more of an empire in the West, and Pyrrhus decided to return to Greece before Antigonus was firmly established on the throne of Macedon. From Tarentum he sent to Pella a demand for subsidies of men and money which was in fact equivalent to a declaration of war;[2] but before following it up he resolved on one more campaign against the Romans on behalf of his Italian allies. Since he did not intend to withdraw from Italy altogether, there was something of policy in this decision, but there was, no doubt, more of pride which made him unwilling to seem to have deserted his allies. In 275 he marched northwards to encounter the consul Dentatus near Beneventum, but the failure of a long encircling movement prevented him from gaining any advantage in the battle,[3] and after it he returned at once to Tarentum. Some nine thousand men— that is about half of what remained of his army after six years of warfare—he left in Italy to garrison the Greek cities of the coast, and with the rest he re-crossed the Straits of Otranto.[4]

[1] Beloch, IV. 1. 556 n. 1. It was this naval disaster and not his difficulties in Italy or Sicily that was the chief cause of Pyrrhus' return to Greece.

[2] Justin, XXV. 3. 1; Pausanias, I. 13. 1–2; Polyaenus, VI. 1. 1.

[3] Beloch, IV. 1. 557 n. 1.

[4] Plutarch, *Pyrrhus*, 24, says that Pyrrhus arrived at Tarentum in 275 with 20,000 foot and 3000 horse. It is, of course, possible that he brought some Sicilian troops with him, but this figure probably represents all that was left of his Greeks—both those that had been in garrison duty in Italy and those that he had brought back from Sicily.

To invade Macedon with an army of fifteen thousand men[1]—and Pyrrhus can have had no more—was a venture which owed its success to the war-weariness of the Macedonian people. They offered no genuine resistance to the Epirot king, who had already ruled over them once before, and Antigonus was forced to have recourse to Gallic mercenaries. Driven from upper Macedonia and from Thessaly, he retained only the coast towns—Thessalonica, Demetrias and the rest—and an attempt which he made in 273 to recover the bulk of his kingdom was defeated by Pyrrhus' son Ptolemaeus, whom his father had appointed to administer the conquered territories. Pyrrhus himself, meanwhile, was preparing for a final campaign, which was to raise the states of the Peloponnese against Antigonus and drive him from his last strongholds.[2] By recalling most of his troops from Italy and impressing a number of Macedonians he was able to get together an army of twenty-five thousand men by the spring of 272. Since the way over the Isthmus was barred to him by Antigonus' garrison at Corinth, he relied on the friendship of the Aetolians to allow him to traverse their territory and to transport his forces across the gulf to Elis and Achaea. We have seen already how the war which had been waged between Gonatas and the Peloponnesian states in the years imme-

Taking into account his losses at Beneventum and the 8500 troops which Plutarch (ch. 26) says that he took back to Greece in 275, this would mean that about 10,000 men were left to guard South Italy, i.e. just about the same number as had been left there during the Sicilian expedition. Most of these were recalled, together with Helenus, to take part in the Peloponnesian campaign (Justin, xxv. 3. 6) and Milo was probably left with little more than the garrison of Tarentum.

[1] Plutarch, *Pyrrhus*, 26; Justin, xxv. 3; Pausanias, I. 13. 2–3. For the numbers, see Appendix V (iv).

[2] Beloch, iv. 1. 574 seq. The years between 288 and 280 had shown Pyrrhus that Antigonus' strength lay in Corinth and Demetrias as much as in Pella, and without a rising of Greece he could never hope to subdue his enemy entirely. His Peloponnesian campaign was not a piece of folly.

diately succeeding 280 had terminated in a series of "agreements" which brought the Macedonian party into power in the various cities. This state of affairs Pyrrhus described in his manifesto as a slavery[1] from which he had come to free the Peloponnesians, and his arrival did, in fact, arouse a measure of anti-Macedonian enthusiasm. No doubt there were many political exiles in his train, all with hopes of their restoration; certainly there was one of note—Cleonymus—whom Pyrrhus intended to escort back to Sparta after he had settled the affairs of Elis, Achaea and Megalopolis. But Cleonymus was not only the enemy of Macedon, he was also the enemy of his nephew King Areus, who had been by no means displeased at his exile four years before and was now determined to oppose his return. An embassy met Pyrrhus at Megalopolis to negotiate while preparations were made for a defence,[2] and when the attack came the Spartans put up a desperate resistance. In the circumstances their courage alone would not have saved them, but help came from a most unusual quarter. Antigonus had moved southwards from Demetrias to Corinth to meet his enemy, and now sent on a force under his general Ameinias to hinder Pyrrhus from the capture of Sparta. Breaking off the assault the Epirot turned northward, and came face to face with Antigonus in the Argolid. The city of Argos lay between their camps, and Pyrrhus, anxious to forestall his rival in securing it, ventured a night

---

[1] Plutarch, *Pyrrhus*, 27.

[2] Pyrrhus' attack on Sparta was described by the pro-Spartan historian Phylarchus, and treated by him as though it was unexpected and constituted a breach of international law. In fact, however, it must have been perfectly clear to everyone in Sparta that he meant to restore Cleonymus, and that if they did not take him back they ran the risk of being attacked. Pyrrhus expected that they would take him back quietly—Plutarch, ch. 27. 3, shows that there was a party favourable to Cleonymus in the city—and it was only when King Areus was actually on his way home from Crete to head the party of resistance that the Epirots delivered their assault.

attack. A gate was opened by partisans inside the walls, the Epirot troops poured in, and there in a turmoil of street fighting their king was killed. His death paralysed the army, and Helenus, who took over the command, did not think of continuing the campaign, while on his side Antigonus had no wish to force a battle by the severity of his terms. The surrender of all Pyrrhus' conquests in Macedon and Thessaly was, of course, an essential condition, but Epirus itself was left intact.[1] The body of Pyrrhus was burned in the market-place at Argos, and his ashes his son and his army brought back with them to Ambracia.

*　*　*　*　*

King Pyrrhus, with his restless energy and adventurous schemes, was a spirit more akin to the immediate successors of Alexander than to the princes who were his contemporaries; and his death closes the period of transition from the world empire of the great conqueror to the well-defined group of hellenistic monarchies. In antiquity his fame, which was considerable, rested in the main on his preeminence as a general, and of late it has been the fashion to deny him any ability off the battle-field. Certainly there was in his statesmanship neither the refinement of Philadelphus nor the infinite patience of Gonatas; but if it has seemed without method, it is in part at least because Pyrrhus' reign has so often been viewed as an incident in the history of other countries than his own—in the annals of Rome, in which he appears a transient and ineffectual figure, striving to stem the inevitable and salutary advance of the Republic, or, in the history of Macedon, a wrongheaded disturber of the preordained rule of the Antigonids.

[1] The terms of the peace between Macedon and Epirus in 272 are nowhere recorded. They have to be deduced from the sequel. They may have been provided for the freedom of Acarnania if that had not been already achieved. See p. 65 and Appendix VIII.

Yet it is as a king of Epirus that he must be judged, and in the light of his country's past history the main lines of his policy were sound enough. With its execution it was different, for there grave faults of temper and still more mischance ruined plans that were in themselves well conceived and made of his life a failure for which there is nothing to be shown. If, indeed, it is nothing to have won the devotion of one's countrymen, and in return to have given them, for the first and last time in their history, a brief moment of fame.

CHAPTER IV

MONARCHY AND REPUBLIC

THE history of the half century which follows the death of Alexander the Great is apt to bewilder the reader by the mass of its detail. By contrast, the fifty years which intervene between the death of Pyrrhus and the point which Polybius chose for the beginning of his work[1] have until recently appeared as an uncharted sea in which a few undated and unrelated facts drifted aimlessly to and fro. But at last the fruit of much labour is ripening. The chronology is becoming fixed, and though details are no doubt lost beyond recovery, the main lines are in general tolerably clear. The reader who has noticed that our knowledge of Epirot history is at best scanty will not be surprised to learn that in these years there is desperately little to record, but what there is may, perhaps, be rendered a little more intelligible by a few general remarks such as I have prefixed to the earlier chapters of this essay.

Towards the middle of the third century it is possible to detect a reaction against monarchy and a revival of republicanism in Greece. The period of bewilderment was over; the nature of hellenistic kingship was by now tolerably clear, and the institution was not acceptable to Greece. Philosophy that had prepared the ground for monarchy in the fourth century contributed little to the political problem in the third. The new schools of Stoics and Epicureans are said to have performed some of the func-

[1] The more or less simultaneous accession to the great hellenistic thrones of three young sovereigns, two of whom were to be conquered by Rome while the third was to leave his country dependent upon the support of the Republic, Philip V of Macedon (221); Antiochus III of Syria (223); Ptolemy IV, Philopator, of Egypt (221).

tions of a religion. Certainly they seem largely to have neglected those of a political philosophy. On occasion the Stoic would face the grandeur of Ptolemy and Seleucid with the unhelpful boast that the true king is the man who is independent of his material surroundings, but of any attempt to restate the case for democracy or to suggest reforms that might bring out the good points of monarchy, there is little or no trace.[1] The Academy, indeed, maintained its founder's interest in the problems of government and in Ecdelos and Demophanes, pupils of Arcesilas who combined the profession of lawgivers with the trade of political assassins, it gave two heroes to the republican movement;[2] but on the whole one may fairly say that that movement lacked an intellectual backing. The monarchs of the Levant were, of course, uninfluenced by it. The most ardent republican was ready enough to take Ptolemy's gold and to flatter Ptolemy's ambassadors, and there was not the least danger of a republican rising in Alexandria or in Antioch. In Pella and Ambracia, however, it was very different, and in both those capitals the people rose, but while timely concessions and the accession of a very able sovereign saved the crown of Macedon, the weaker crown of Epirus went down for ever in the republican storm.[3]

Pyrrhus' eldest son, Ptolemaeus, had been killed in the assault at Sparta, and though he had himself left a son, a baby was no fit king for the Epirots in this time of difficulty. In his place Alexander, Pyrrhus' son by Lanassa, was called to the throne and made what amends he could to the rights of primogeniture by adopting his little nephew.[4]

[1] It is a commonplace of the books that in the hellenistic age "individual ethics" became of the first importance in philosophy. The larger field was to some extent neglected by the new schools.

[2] For their exploits in Sicyon, Megalopolis and Cyrene see Beloch, IV. 1. 614 seq.

[3] For the republican movement in general see Beloch, IV. 1, ch. 17.

[4] See Appendix VII, p. 127.

The new king had been destined by his father for the throne of Sicily, but to maintain his claim to be Agathocles' heir was now quite out of his power, and one of his first acts as king in Epirus was to recall Milo and his garrison from Tarentum, and thus to proclaim that he had no thought of renewing Pyrrhus' Western enterprise. He seems, however, not to have severed all connection with Syracuse but to have kept on friendly terms with those who had supported his father's rule there—in particular with a certain Hieron, who was soon to take for himself the kingship which Alexander had resigned.[1] Of events in Epirus in the first years of the new reign we know only of a campaign against the Illyrians, who had hoped, no doubt, to use the opportunity of Pyrrhus' death to recover some of the territory that he had taken from them.[2] Meanwhile in Greece the Acarnanians were now free of Epirot control while the Aetolians remained, as before, friends of Epirus.[3]

An equilibrium of power between the three great hellenistic monarchies could only subsist if no one of the kings was in effective control of Greece, and we have seen already how any king of Macedon who threatened to gain such a control invariably encountered there a resistance subsidised from abroad. It had been so with Cassander, and with Demetrius, and now within seven years of Pyrrhus' death the gold of Egypt built up a coalition of Greek states, under the joint leadership of Athens and

[1] Justin, XXIII. 3. 3 (where Alexander is confused with Helenus); Beloch, IV. 2. 276. Hieron had been a supporter of Pyrrhus (Justin, XXIII. 4. 13; Pausanias, VI. 12. 2) and his continued friendship with Alexander is evidenced by the marriage of his son to the Epirot princess Nereis about 235. See p. 96.

[2] Trogus, *Prologue*, 25. For Pyrrhus and the Illyrians, see Beloch, IV. 2. 381.

[3] For the relations of the Aetolians and Acarnanians with one another and with Epirus at this date see Appendix VIII.

Sparta,[1] which involved Antigonus in the lengthy conflict known as the "Chremonidean" War. It would have been well for the king of Epirus to have taken no part in it and to have allowed his kingdom a longer time to recover from the effects of Pyrrhus' ambition, but he could not resist what seemed a golden opportunity, and an Epirot army invaded Macedon while Antigonus was occupied with the siege of Athens.[2] No doubt Alexander looked for a success such as had attended his father's invasion of 274, but Pyrrhus had been a general of quite exceptional ability and further, ten years of Antigonus' rule had taught the Macedonians that they had a king for whom it was worth while to fight. So the Epirots were routed at Derdia, and when Antigonus' generals followed up their victory by invading Epirus in their turn, Alexander abandoned his kingdom and took refuge with the Acarnanians.

Here was a situation curiously parallel to that which had

[1] The inscription recording the alliance between Athens and Sparta has been preserved (*Syll.*[3] 434–5). It is worth noticing that no one who read it without a knowledge of the history of the time would guess that the "Areus" whose name occurs so often was one of the kings of Sparta. That Sparta had kings he would know, for they are mentioned though not named; but he would think that Areus was some independent prince who led the allied forces, but himself stood outside the alliance. This fact is of interest in view of what was said in chapter II (p. 27) as to the "hegemon" standing outside the "symmachy". Coins were issued at Sparta for the first time in these years. Some of them bear the inscription "Βασίλεος Ἄρεος" but none the name of the other king, Eudamidas. It is fairly clear that he was completely overshadowed by his colleague. Lambros (*Peloponnese*, Pl. IA'. 6).

[2] Justin, XXVI. 2. 9, places Alexander's invasion of Macedon during the Chremonidean War, i.e. between spring 266 and autumn 262. Tarn—*C.A.H.* VII. 708—accepts this dating, but Beloch—IV. 2. 504—remarking, with justice, that Justin's chronology is almost worthless, gives some reasons for preferring to date the invasion about 258 and to bring it into relation with the campaign of King Acrotatus of Sparta which he would put in that year. Cf. IV. 1. 597. In Appendix VI I have tried to show that Acrotatus' death must itself fall before 261.

arisen on the flight of King Aeacides in 317, and now Antigonus followed Cassander's example in abolishing the
Molossian monarchy—the keystone of Epirot unity—and
leaving the various tribal assemblies to carry on the
government of the country. In one respect, indeed, he
seems to have gone further than his model, for it appears
that he also abolished the Epirot confederacy and its
delegate assembly. In this step his object was, of course,
to break up Epirus into its component tribes, but the land
had been a unity for too long for such a scheme to succeed,
and it is probable that within quite a few years the Molossian tribal assembly had assimilated some, at least, of the
other tribes by granting them "sympolity" with itself—in
this way creating a closer union than had existed before.[1]
Nor was it only to their unity that the Epirots were attached.
Many of them, especially among the Molossians, were still
royalist and wished for their king again—a wish which
was backed by the support of the Aetolians to whom
King Alexander was naturally preferable to a republican
government under the influence of Macedon. With their
help[2] Alexander regained his throne sometime in the
decade between 260 and 250, but both the exact date
and the circumstances of the restoration are matters
for conjecture. One may think, perhaps, that Antigonus
gave his assent to it as a gesture of conciliation and modera-
tion in the hour of his triumph after his victory over the
Egyptian fleet off Cos; or again that he was forced to
acquiesce in it some five years later when the superb

[1] See p. 46 above and Appendix IV below. *S.G.D.I.* 1334, 1335,
1337 show a "koinon" of the Molossians which included parts of
Epirus outside the proper boundaries of Molossia. This is best explained by supposing that these other parts asked for "sympolity"
with the Molossians, and in *S.G.D.I.* 1590 we perhaps have evidence of
such a request.

[2] Justin, XXVI. 3. 1, where the "socii" are probably the Aetolians,
and perhaps the Acarnanians as well. See also Appendix VIII.

diplomacy of Philadelphus had redeemed the failure of his admirals and paralysed the whole system of his adversary's policy.[1]

By 250 at the latest Alexander was once more king in Epirus, but his position there was no longer what it had been before his exile. We have seen how the condition of the survival of the Molossian kingship into the fourth century had been the limited nature of its powers, and how Pyrrhus in the spirit of his time converted it in practice into an autocracy. It is natural to suppose that Alexander in the first part of his reign ruled as his father had ruled before him, but in the interval of his exile the latent republicanism of the Epirots revived and on his return he was forced to compromise with it. The Molossian tribal assembly continued to exercise the functions of government jointly with the king, whose name appeared at the head of its decrees as that of the chief officer of the state. Epirus was in fact a constitutional monarchy.[2]

After his victory Antigonus had taken from Epirus the border provinces of Tymphaea and Parauaea which Pyrrhus had acquired in 294[3]. This was a serious loss of territory,

[1] Philadelphus' diplomacy brought about the revolt of Alexander, son of Craterus, Antigonus' governor in Corinth (c. 252), and also a change of alliances by which Syria, which had been allied to Macedon since 278 (see p. 80 above), became for a while the ally of Egypt. This was an achievement comparable to that of Prince Kaunitz, and it is interesting—if irrelevant—to notice that the pledge of the new alliance, the Egyptian Princess Berenice, met in Antioch a fate as horrible as befell "L'Autrichienne" in Paris. See Tarn, *Antigonos Gonatas*, p. 376.

[2] *S.G.D.I.* 1334, 1335, 1337, and Appendix IV. A question arises here. These are inscriptions of the Molossian "koinon":—are we to suppose (a) that this "koinon" had absorbed all the other tribal assemblies, or (b) that there were other "koina" in Epirus which counted Alexander as their king, or (c) that on his return he regained only his Molossian crown? There is not enough evidence to answer these questions.

[3] See p. 59 above. Tarn, *Antigonos Gonatas*, pp. 311–12, and Beloch, IV. 2. 379. As to Atintania, it would certainly be natural to suppose that

but soon after his restoration Alexander compensated himself for it in a fashion which did him no credit. Since their rise to power at the time of the Gallic invasion, the Aetolians had steadily extended the boundaries of their federation, and in these years it was their chief desire to incorporate in it the Acarnanians, who had been their allies for some years now, but were nevertheless unwilling to sacrifice their independence to them. This people had, of course, every claim on Alexander's gratitude, yet he was not ashamed to join with the Aetolians in a partition of their land[1] which added its western portion and the island of Leucas to his kingdom. Epirus was not at all benefited by this violation of the decencies of politics, for within a few years the death of Alexander[2] cut short all hope of the country regaining the position of a great power. His nephew, Pyrrhus the younger, had died shortly before him, and now the kingship descended to Pyrrhus' son Ptolemaeus, a boy about ten years old for whom Alexander's queen Olympias acted as regent. She was unpopular in the country—indeed it was rumoured that she had poisoned her nephew to attain the regency—and in her rule the Aetolians saw

Antigonus took this province too, and that Antigoneia on the Aous was an Antigonid foundation; but—*pace* Tarn—Polybius, II. 5, goes far to show that the country belonged to Epirus in 229, and since it can hardly have been recovered between 260 and 230, one is forced to conclude that Antigonus did not take it after Alexander's defeat.

[1] The literary references to the partition of Acarnania between the Aetolians and Alexander give no indication of its date (Polybius, II. 45. 1, IX. 34. 7; Justin, XXVI. 3. 1, XXVIII. 1. 1). It is usual to date it about 265, but against this one may urge (a) that it is too near to the Aetolian-Acarnanian treaty printed in Syll.³ 421, (b) that Justin (XXVI. 2. 9) speaks as though Alexander went into exile among the Acarnanians whereas, if 265 is right for the partition, he returned from one part of his dominions to another, (c) it is hard to believe that Antigonus would have allowed Alexander to remain in possession of his ill-gotten gains between 262 and 252. See also Appendix VIII.

[2] For the date of Alexander's death, and the events which followed upon it in Epirus, see Appendix VII.

an opportunity to acquire that half of Acarnania which had fallen to the share of Alexander and even, perhaps, to add Epirus itself to their league.

After the Chremonidean War which had been marked by two defeats of Sparta and had ended in the fall of Athens, the leadership of the opposition to the Macedonian power passed from those cities to two federations which had grown up among the tribes of Aetolia and the cities of Achaea, parts of Greece that before the third century had had little share in their country's history.[1] The tribes of Epirus were themselves linked together by a federal bond, but their federation was as it were crowned with a king. When Epirots saw their neighbours in Aetolia growing constantly in strength, extending the bounds of their league and as it were championing the cause of republicanism against the Macedonian monarchy, it was natural that many of them should be influenced to think of ridding their country of an anomalous encumbrance and should forget that their monarchy might perhaps be the safeguard of their independence. The Molossians themselves probably remained loyal to the royal house, but the country as a whole had not been welded together for so long a time that the other Epirots could look upon the monarchy as their own, and in the capital at Ambracia the dynasty was definitely unpopular. In these circumstances there broke out soon after the death of King Alexander a war between the Aetolian and Achaean leagues on the one side and the monarchies of Epirus and Macedon on the other.[2] The details of the struggle are extremely obscure, but it is evident that Olympias soon found herself hard pressed by the Aetolians and appealed for help to the courts of Pella

---

[1] In general see *C.A.H.* VII, ch. 23 (Tarn), and Beloch, IV. I, ch. 20.
[2] The so-called "Demetrian War"—*C.A.H.* VII. 744 seq. and Beloch, IV. I. 630 seq.—may perhaps be regarded as a contest between the opposing principles of monarchism and republicanism.

and—strangely enough—of Syracuse. Her daughter Phthia was married to King Demetrius of Macedon,[1] and her niece Nereis—a few years later—to Hieron's son the crown prince Gelon;[2] but neither union advantaged her much. From Sicily there came only a force of Gallic mercenaries who were so little to be trusted that Hieron was glad to be rid of them,[3] while Demetrius was too hard pressed himself to send anything to his mother-in-law. Indeed after his death following hard upon a serious reverse at the hands of the barbarian tribesmen on the northern frontier it needed all the ability of his successor Antigonus Doson to save the Macedonian monarchy,[4] and meanwhile the Epirot monarchy had fallen. The details of its fall are mainly to seek. We know that the young king Ptolemaeus was assassinated in Ambracia and we can guess that the Gauls turned traitors. Olympias died, of grief, as it is said: and finally the princess Deidameia, the last of the Aeacidae, was driven by the mob to take refuge in the temple of Artemis and there brutally murdered. To seal the downfall of the monarchy the Ambraciots broke open the tomb of King Pyrrhus and scattered his ashes through the streets of the capital.[5]

[1] Justin, XXVIII. 1. 1. For the date, see Tarn, *Classical Quarterly*, 1924, 18.

[2] Justin, XXVIII. 3. 4. For the chronology, which is quite uncertain, see Appendix VII.

[3] Polybius, II. 7. It seems to me likely that these Gauls were originally sent to Epirus to help the dynasty.

[4] It appears from Justin, XXVIII. 3. 9, that Doson at the beginning of his reign was faced with a serious revolutionary movement in Macedon. I take it that the alteration in the royal style from Βασιλεὺς Ἀντίγονος Μακεδών to Βασιλεὺς Ἀντίγονος καὶ Μακεδόνες (cf. S.G.D.I. 1368) and the setting up of a "koinon" of the Macedonians (Tarn, *Antigonos Gonatas*, p. 54 n.) were concessions made to republican feeling.

[5] Justin, XXVIII. 3; Polyaenus, VIII. 52; Ovid, *Ibis*, 307–10. One must remember that Ambracia was no part of Molossia and owed no loyalty to the royal house.

The final disappearance of the kingship in Epirus seems to have put an end to the predominance of the Molossians. The monarchy was, of course, in origin a Molossian monarchy, and we have seen how in the reign of Alexander the "koinon" of the Molossians was the chief, if not the only legislative assembly in the land: but now, after the fall of the Aeacids, there appeared for the first time a "koinon" of the Epirots, while the seat of government was moved to Phoenice on the Chaonian coast, far outside the borders of Molossia.[1] The new republic naturally began life in alliance with the Aetolians to whom it owed its existence, but when that people was able to offer them no effectual protection against the incursions of the Illyrian allies of King Demetrius, who came near to destroying them altogether,[2] the Epirots swallowed their republican pride and made their peace with Macedon. In this manner they came, a few years later, to be members of King Antigonus Doson's alliance and sent a contingent to fight at Sellasia.[3]

There was still half a century of independence left for the Epirots, but these years they spent in the shadow of the encroaching power of Rome. The senate had begun to intervene in the lands to the east of the Adriatic soon after the conclusion of the first war with Carthage,[4] and during the course of the second the Romans were for some years at war with King Philip—the successor of Antigonus Doson. Its position midway between Macedon and Italy

[1] *S.G.D.I.* 1338–9. It is to be noted that the "prostates" of the Molossians survived as an official of the Epirot league.

[2] Polybius, II. 4–6. It must have been at this time that the Illyrians acquired Atintania: compare Polybius, II. 5. 8 with II. 11. 11 and Appian, *Illyr.* 7.

[3] Polybius, II. 65. 4.

[4] The appeal of the Acarnanians to Rome recorded by Justin, xxviii. 1–2, *c.* 235 B.C., is rejected as fictitious by Holleaux, *Les Monarchies hellénistiques*, p. 7, but is accepted as genuine by Beloch, with whom I agree. The Illyrian War of 228 was the first armed intervention of Rome to the east of the Adriatic.

made Epirus the principal seat of operations, and in these circumstances it was the natural and proper policy of those who controlled the affairs of the country to strive for peace. The treaty which ended the first Macedonian war was brought about to a great extent by the Epirots and was actually signed in their capital city.[1] Similarly in the second war between Rome and Philip they did their best to effect a peaceful settlement;[2] but this time they were unsuccessful, and, as a result of Philip's defeat at Cynoscephalae, they were compelled to enter the Roman alliance.[3] Inevitably there grew up two parties in the state—the friends of Macedon and those of Rome—and, unfortunately, in the years in which the third and final conflict between the two great powers was brewing, each party in Epirus was headed by an enthusiastic partisan. The dissensions between Charops and Antinous of Clathiatus divided the people, and when at last war came, the more popular Antinous was able to persuade the majority of the Epirots—including nearly all the Molossians—to desert Rome in favour of King Perseus.[4]

It was, of course, a disastrous decision, and after the Roman victory it was natural enough that the praetor Anicius should come to see to the punishment of the leaders who had been responsible for it.[5] But, meanwhile, the senate at home had determined to take a more extensive vengeance, and Aemilius Paullus, the victor of Pydna, received the order to reward his legions at the expense of the Epirots. The spirit in which these instructions were carried out sent a shudder of horror through the Greek world, for in the space of a few weeks seventy towns were sacked and a multitude of the inhabitants deported into

---

[1] Livy, XXIX. 12; Polybius, XVIII. 1. 14.
[2] Livy, XXXII. 10 and XXXII. 14. 5.
[3] Livy XXXV. 27. 11 and, generally, *C.A.H.* VIII, ch. 5.
[4] Polybius, XXVII. 13–14, XXX. 7. 2.   [5] Livy, XLV. 26.

slavery.[1] That was the end of Epirus. "In time past", says Strabo, "the land though mountainous was well populated, but now it is for the most part a wilderness with here and there a decaying village."[2] "Solitudinem faciunt, pacem appellant" is the inevitable thought, and there is much in the rise of Rome to justify it, for the great republic attained to world supremacy when she was still quite unfitted for the tasks of world rule. A time was to come, no doubt, when men could speak with a show of justice of the boundless majesty of Roman peace, but first the lessons of government had to be learnt and in the learning of them the schoolroom—the whole Mediterranean world—became only too often, like Dante's Italy, a hostelry of pain; of pain that might well have been spared it if Philip, the son of Amyntas, had lived to unite Greece with Macedon.

[1] Plutarch, *Aemilius*, 29; Polybius, xxx. 15. 5; Livy, xlv. 34. Many of the "πόλεις" were no doubt mere hill-fortresses with a very small permanent population, and the figure of 150,000 given by the contemporary Polybius as the number of the captives, if not entirely inconsistent with the huge demand for slaves at that time, can hardly be reconciled with a modern estimate of the total population of Epirus in antiquity (Beloch. iii. 1. 293). Nevertheless, there is no reason to doubt that the Roman "pacification" effected the ruin of the country.

[2] Strabo, vii. 327; generally *C.A.H.* viii, ch. 8. 5.

APPENDIX I

THE DESCENDANTS OF ACHILLES

THERE was considerable diversity and often some inconsistency in the various accounts which existed in antiquity of the fortunes of Achilles' son Neoptolemus after the fall of Troy. All these accounts can be found in Roscher's *Lexicon of Mythology* under the heading "Neoptolemus"; the only purpose of this Appendix is to trace the development of that version which made him the ancestor of the Molossian kings.

In Homer there is no hint of a connection between Neoptolemus and Epirus.[1] This legend seems to have made its first appearance[2] in the *Nostoi* of Hagias of Troezen—a cyclic epic dated about 800—but since our knowledge of the poem is derived from a short epitome, it is difficult to say what form it took.[3] Probably it made Neoptolemus sojourn among the Molossians for a short time on his return journey from Troy before he reached his home in Thessaly, and did not imply that subsequent kings of the Molossians were descended from him.[4] This addition appears for the first time in an ode of Pindar—written about 485—and though it is not necessary to suppose that the poet himself was responsible for the genealogy, I do not think that it can have been current for many years before that date.[5]

[1] Regard, for instance, *Odyssey*, III. 189.

[2] It may be asked, why was Epirus ever thought of in connection with Neoptolemus? Perhaps it was a recollection of what lies behind *Iliad*, XVI. 233.

[3] Proculus, *Chrestomathia*. Apollodorus, *Epitome*, VI. 12, may contain material derived from the *Nostoi*, but it is impossible to say how much.

[4] Wilamowitz (*Pindaros*, p. 167) says that Pindar is "the first to make Neoptolemus come among the Molossians", and neglects the *Nostoi* altogether. It does seem, however, that N.'s "Nostos" ended in Thessaly and involved only a short stay in Epirus (Pearson, *Fragments of Sophocles*, II. 140). Therefore Farnell—*Hero Cults*, p. 314—is probably wrong in saying that the Molossian kings claimed descent from Neoptolemus as early as the eighth century.

[5] *Nemean*, VII. 39. The Molossians can only recently have attained a position in Epirus which would justify such a claim. Wilamowitz describes it as "schwerlich alt".

Pindar does not give any hint as to how the connection between the hero and the kings of historical times was established, but Proxenos—the third-century historian of Epirus—records that the royal family traced its descent back to "Pielos, son of Neoptolemus, whom they also call Peleus". This suggests that Pielos was their old barbarian ancestor and that the resemblance which his name bore to Peleus enabled him to be put forward as a son of Neoptolemus when the royal family felt cultured enough to claim hellenic descent.[1]

The next reference to the genealogy is contained in the *Andromache* of Euripides (c. 420). This play is based on a tradition which made Neoptolemus return from Troy to Thessaly direct, and according to it the connection between his house and Molossia began only after his death, when his concubine Andromache, and Helenus, a son of Priam, removed from Thessaly to Epirus, and Andromache's son by Neoptolemus became king of the Molossians.[2]

This form of the legend is obviously inconsistent with that given by Pindar, but it is interesting to note that the figure of Helenus which it supplied was soon put to a useful political purpose. It was said that he migrated to Chaonia, when Neoptolemus' son grew old enough to rule for himself in Molossia, and became the ancestor of the Chaonian royal family. This development of the story is probably to be dated about 380 when King Alcetas was endeavouring to draw the two tribes together. Olympias, the mother of Alexander the Great (born about 375), claimed to be descended from Achilles and Helenus, and the latter claim suggests that her father, Neoptolemus, was married to a princess of Chaonia in furtherance of Alcetas' policy.[3]

[1] Schol. ad Eur. *Androm.* 32 with Schwartz' correction as given in Roscher s.v. "Pielos". Justin, XVII. 3. 8, and Pausanias, I. 11. 2 (? both derived from Proxenos) also mention Pielos as the original ancestor of the royal family. Cf. *S.G.D.I.* 1352, where the royal clan (Pielis) is mentioned and Fick makes the Pielos-Peleus suggestion.

[2] Eur. *Androm.* 1243 seq. For the political significance of the play see p. 12 n. 4. It is to be noted that Andromache's son is not named in the play: it is only in the late dramatis personae that he is called Molossus.

[3] Pausanias, I. 11. 2. For Olympias' claim: Theopompus in schol. to Lycophron, 1439. Koehler (*Sat. Phil. Sauppio obl.* p. 83) has suggested how it arose. See also p. 32 above.

The last stage in the development of the genealogy comes in the third century and is manifested in a variety of ways.

(1) The fame of King Pyrrhus led to an almost universal substitution of "Pyrrhus" for "Neoptolemus" in the tradition. Pyrrhus appears as early as the *Cypria* as an alternative name for Achilles' son, but until King Aeacides thought of giving the name to his son in 320 it does not appear to have been much used. After that Neoptolemus tended to give place to it.[1]

(2) Hitherto the tradition of descent from Achilles had been personal to the royal family. Their claim was that Neoptolemus, a Thessalian, had come among the Molossians, ruled over them and bequeathed his crown to his descendants. But in the third century—when the Epirots in general were regarded as Greeks—the tradition was broadened by making the tribal hero "Molossus" a son of Neoptolemus. Sometimes, indeed, he is spoken of as his only son, but in the better genealogies as a brother of Pielos, on whom, it will be remembered, the royal clan depended for their personal claim.[2]

(3) As well as his children by Andromache, Neoptolemus was now endowed with a large family by Lanassa, a granddaughter of Heracles. This princess was brought into the tradition out of respect to Lanassa, the daughter of Agathocles of Syracuse, King Pyrrhus' second wife and the mother of King Alexander II. Her relationship with Heracles accorded well with King Pyrrhus' claim to the throne of Macedon.[3]

[1] Pyrrhus in the *Cypria:* Pausanias, x. 26. 4. Usener's statement (*Archiv f. Rel. Wiss.* 1904, pp. 330–31) that in Epirus Achilles' son was always Pyrrhus neglects most of the evidence, e.g. that of Pindar.

[2] See Strabo (ch. 326) where the royal family is called "Thessalian" and distinguished from the "native" kings of the neighbouring tribes. Molossus was the eponymous hero of the tribe and at first had nothing to do with the royal genealogy. When the distinction between the Greek king and his barbarian people had vanished, Molossus became a son of Neoptolemus; but Pausanias (I. 11. 2) is careful to emphasise that though Molossus ruled the country after Neoptolemus' death, it was from Pielos that the royal house was descended. Later Pielos was dropped and Molossus son of Neoptolemus was made the sole ancestor, e.g. Eustathius, schol. ad *Odyss.* III. 189. Klotzsch (in the appendix to his *History*) has argued in the contrary sense—that Molossus was the original son of Neoptolemus and that Pielos was added later. This seems to me very unlikely.

[3] Schol. ad Eur. *Androm.* 24; Plutarch, *Pyrrhus,* 1; Justin, XVII. 3. 4.

APPENDIX II

DIONYSIUS AND ALCETAS

OUR knowledge of the relations of Dionysius of Syracuse with King Alcetas depends on a passage of Diodorus (xv. 13) and an inscription (*I.G.* II². 101 = *Syll.*³ 154). The interpretation of them given in the text must be justified.

(1) Diodorus' account is fairly straightforward. Dionysius wanted to have an ally on the Greek mainland and restored Alcetas against the wishes of the Molossians. What is not clear is the attitude of the Spartans to the restoration, for one cannot tell whether the force which they sent to aid the Molossians was directed solely against the Illyrians or against the Illyrians and Alcetas. In any case Alcetas regained his throne and must have become a close ally of Dionysius to whom he owed it. Meyer[1] is confident that he also became an ally of Sparta, but I cannot see that Dionysius had anything to gain by forcing him to take this step, and Alcetas' own inclinations were obviously anti-Spartan.

(2) The inscription runs:

> ἐπὶ Ἀστείο ἄρχοντος
> Ἀλκέτο τοῦ Λεπτίνο Συρακοσίο
> Ἀκαμαντὶς ἐπρυτάνευε
> Θουδαίτης Διομειεὺς ἐγραμμάτευε.

Underneath these words, which are inscribed at the head of a "stele", appears the bas-relief of a horse—the emblem of Syracuse—and underneath the horse part of an olive crown. The substance of the inscription, which came below the crown, is lost, but the "stele" evidently commemorated the bestowal of a crown on "Alcetas, son of Leptines, of Syracuse".[2] Asteios was archon in the year 373/2, but the prytany-month of the Acamantid tribe is, unfortunately, unknown.

Two questions must be raised: (1) the identity of Alcetas, (2) the relations between Athens and Syracuse in Asteios' year.

---

[1] Meyer, *Geschichte des Altertums*, v. 299.
[2] See Foucart in *Bull. Corr. Hell.* XII. 177.

(1) It is agreed that the Leptines of the inscription was almost certainly Dionysius' brother who was himself honoured by the Athenians in 394/3, for the bestowal of a crown was in 373 still a rare honour reserved for high rank or great services, and no other Leptines of Syracuse is known to us at this date.[1] It is also agreed that Alcetas is not a name which one would readily associate with Syracuse or the house of Dionysius, and that it is probably to be brought into connection with the exile of Alcetas the Molossian at the tyrant's court. The connection which is usually suggested is that Leptines named his son Alcetas in honour of the exile.[2] Since it is very improbable that the Alcetas of the inscription was born after 395, the king of the Molossians must, in this case, have been in exile for a long period, and it is hard to believe that at a time (i.e. c. 395) when there was no immediate hope of his restoration, he was of sufficient importance at the court of Syracuse to give a name to the tyrant's nephew. But a far graver objection to the general view is the fact that Alcetas of Molossia paid a visit to Athens in Asteios' year and did the Athenians a service about this time which might well entitle him to the honour of a crown. It would be, I think, in these circumstances, a most remarkable coincidence if the Alcetas of the inscription and Alcetas of Molossia were namesakes, and not—as Dittmar has suggested—the same person.[3] Dionysius may well have desired to attach Alcetas to himself by causing him to be adopted into his family, and I have suggested in the text that the reason why Alcetas used this Syracusan citizenship and parentage on his visit to Athens in 373 was that he was then "more or less the envoy of Dionysius".[4] This brings us to the second question—that of the relations between Dionysius and Athens in these years.

(2) In 373/2 Athens was at war with Sparta, and although the exact nature of the alliance between Sparta and Dionysius is unknown, Iphicrates' action in seizing the Syracusan triremes at Corcyra seems to show that his city was at war with the tyrant as

[1] *Syll.*[3] 128: Dittmar, *de Atheniensium more exteros coronis ornandi* (Leipzig, 1890), p. 196.

[2] Foucart (*ubi supra*); Klotzsch, p. 36.

[3] Demosthenes, *c. Timotheum*, 22; Xenophon, *Hell.* VI. 2. 10; Dittmar, *op. cit.* p. 197.

[4] P. 36 above.

well. Dionysius complained of the sacrilege involved in this capture, and Beloch and others have suggested—I think quite rightly—that the Alcetas of the inscription was the envoy who brought his complaint to Athens.[1] Even if Beloch was willing to identify the two Alcetas—which he is not[2]—his chronology for these years would make it impossible for him to identify the two appearances at Athens—(1) as an advocate for Timotheus, (2) as an envoy from Dionysius—since he dates Iphicrates' expedition in the spring of 372, several months after Timotheus' trial, but there are, in my opinion, good reasons for thinking that the seizure of the tyrant's triremes took place about September 373, and if this is so Alcetas might easily be in a position to complain of it in Athens in November. It remains to deal with the chronology.

The only certain date is that of Timotheus' trial, which came on in November 373—Demosthenes, c. *Timotheum*, 22. Beloch (III. 2. 234–5) puts his deposition and the beginning of the siege of Corcyra in the autumn of 373, the arrival of the relief force in mid-winter and Iphicrates' expedition in the spring of 372. He is led to this view mainly by his belief that Iphicrates was present at his predecessor's trial at Athens; but the passage on which he relied (c. *Timotheum*, 13) refers to the accusations which caused Timotheus to be deposed and not to the trial itself, and in any case it would have been possible for Iphicrates to sail to Corcyra in the late summer, and return himself for the trial in November. On the other hand, Xenophon's account definitely implies that Corcyra was already in difficulties in the summer of 373; that the Athenians were afraid that Timotheus would not relieve it in that year (ἀναλοῦν τὸν τῆς ὥρας εἰς τὸν περίπλουν χρόνον), and therefore deposed him in favour of Iphicrates, who at once (μάλα ὀξέως) got together a scratch fleet and sailed round the Peloponnese, i.e. about September 373. Cary (*C.A.H.* VI. 77) agrees with this view, though he gives no reasons for it, but Marshall (*Second Athenian Confederacy*, p. 68) follows Beloch's chronology.

[1] Diodorus, XV. 47. 7 and XVI. 57. 3; Beloch, III. 1. 162 n. 1.
[2] Beloch, *loc. cit.* "Wie man in diesem Alcetas den König Alcetas von Epeiros sehen kann, übersteigt die Grenzen meines Begriffsvermögen."

APPENDIX III

KING NEOPTOLEMUS, SON OF ALEXANDER

WE learn from Plutarch (*Pyrrhus*, 4–5) that between 302 and 298 a certain Neoptolemus was king of the Molossians. His name shows that he was a member of the royal house and the circumstances of the time that he was a puppet in the hands of Cassander;[1] but Plutarch tells us nothing of his parentage. It is, however, generally supposed that he was a son of Alexander the Molossian and Cleopatra, and therefore born about 334 B.C.[2] The evidence for this view is twofold.

(1) There is an inscription dated in the reign of King Neoptolemus, son of Alexander,[3] and of this it is said (*a*) that Neoptolemus is the man mentioned by Plutarch, for the only other Neoptolemus who reigned in Molossia was the son of Alcetas, and (*b*) that his father Alexander is evidently King Alexander I.

(2) Plutarch (*Pyrrhus*, 2) says that when Aeacides was driven out in 317 the Molossians "brought in the sons of Neoptolemus" (ἐπηγάγοντο τοὺς Νεοπτολέμου παῖδας). Plutarch does not say who this Neoptolemus was, but Beloch has "emended" the passage into "τοὺς ⟨Ἀλεξάνδρου τοῦ⟩ Νεοπτολέμου παῖδας" in order to get a reference to children of Alexander the Molossian.[4]

This is clearly a very thin case. Argument (2) is of no value, for there is no reason for the emendation. The Neoptolemus of Plutarch, may be the man mentioned in Arrian (II. 27. 6) and Plutarch, *Eumenes*, 4. As to argument (1), if the Neoptolemus of the inscription is the Neoptolemus of Plutarch,

---

[1] E.g. Cassander's operations against Corcyra *c.* 300 B.C. (Diodorus, XXI. 2) could not have been carried out unless he had virtual control of Epirus.

[2] This view seems to have been put forward by Droysen. It is accepted by Niese, I. 348; Beloch, IV. 2. 144; Klotzsch, p. 84; Schmidt, p. 58; *C.A.H.* VI. 464. Reuss (*Rheinisches Museum*, 1881, p. 168) dissents and Schubert (p. 107) is inclined to agree with him.

[3] It is *S.G.D.I.* 1336.

[4] Beloch, IV. 2. 144.

it does not in the least follow that his father was King Alexander the Molossian; he may, for instance, have been the son of Alcetas II mentioned in Diodorus, xix. 88. Conversely, if the Alexander of the inscription is King Alexander I, his son King Neoptolemus may have died when he was a child and have nothing to do with the Neoptolemus of Plutarch.

Now there are, I think, good reasons for saying that if King Alexander the Molossian had a son the child died before 325 and cannot be identified with the Neoptolemus of Plutarch.

(a) Alexander's widow Cleopatra did not remain in Epirus for long after her husband's death. First she moved to Macedon (c. 325) and then on to Sardis (322) and all the time "on account of the splendour of her descent Cassander and Lysimachus, Antigonus and Ptolemy, in a word all those who were after Alexander's death the most distinguished among the generals, were suitors for her hand".[1] Eventually—in 308—Antigonus had to have her executed for fear that she should attach herself to Ptolemy. It is equally difficult to believe that she deserted her little son when she moved from Dodona to Pella or that she took him with her away from his Molossian throne.

(b) In view of what Diodorus says about Cleopatra, it is clear that her son would have been a person of the very greatest importance, especially after the extinction of the direct descendants of Alexander the Great; yet we hear nothing of him until 302 B.C. We are to believe that he remained in continuous possession of at least a share of the Molossian throne from 330 to 302, although Diodorus, who describes the vicissitudes of Epirot history in some detail,[2] never mentions him.

(c) Arrian and Dexippus[3] both speak of Epirus as forming part of Antipater's governorship after Alexander's death. Now it is true that in practice King Philip could have done as he liked with Epirus and Molossia, but in theory they were both of them independent of Macedon, and if Alexander the Molossian left a son who was alive at the death of Alexander the Great, it is

[1] Diodorus, xx. 37. 3. See also for Cleopatra, Plutarch, *Alexander*, 68, and *Eumenes*, 8, and Beloch, IV. 1. 365, who yet believes that Neoptolemus was her son.

[2] E.g. Diodorus, xix. 11. 36. 89.

[3] Arrian, "τὰ μετ' Ἀλέξανδρον" ap. Photius, *Bibl. Cod.* 92; Dexippus, *F.G.H.* (Jacoby), c. 8. 1.

hard to see how Antipater can have administered them officially. But if Alexander the Molossian left no son who survived, then his crown would pass to Olympias and Alexander the Great, and Epirus would come to form part of the Macedonian Empire.

(d) Syncellus (p. 578) preserves a note that the last six Epirot kings reigned for ninety years. The fall of the monarchy is to be dated between 235 and 231 (it cannot possibly be as early as 240) and it is fairly clear that he is reckoning from the death of Alexander the Great and the Lamian War, when Aeacides became king.[1] If, however, the Neoptolemus who, Plutarch says, was reigning in 300 began his reign in 330, then the basis of Syncellus' calculation is entirely destroyed.

It seems, then, that the Neoptolemus of 302 to 297 is not to be identified with a son of Alexander the Molossian, and that if the inscription (Collitz, 1336) refers to him, his father Alexander was some one else; while, if the father is Alexander the Molossian, his son died before 325. In the text I have chosen the former alternative because " $\dot{\epsilon}\pi\grave{\iota}$ $\beta a\sigma\iota\lambda\epsilon os$ $N\epsilon o\pi\tau o\lambda\acute{\epsilon}\mu o\upsilon$ $\langle\beta a\sigma\iota\lambda\epsilon os\rangle$ $A\lambda\epsilon\xi\acute{a}\nu\delta\rho o\upsilon$ " and not " $\dot{\epsilon}\pi\grave{\iota}$ $\beta a\sigma\iota\lambda\epsilon os$ $N\epsilon o\pi\tau o\lambda\acute{\epsilon}\mu o\upsilon$ $A\lambda\epsilon\xi\acute{a}\nu\delta\rho o\upsilon$ " would be the correct style if the father Alexander had been a king:[2] but this is a precarious argument.

---

[1] Cf. p. 43 above, and p. 126 below.
[2] Cf. Dittenberger, *Syll.*[3] 369 and Roussel, *Bull. Corr. Hell.* (1923), p. 30.

APPENDIX IV

SOME INSCRIPTIONS FROM DODONA

THOSE of the inscriptions found at Dodona which record decisions of Molossian or Epirot legislative bodies, and yet can be dated with some confidence in the period before the fall of the monarchy (*c.* 232), divide themselves into three classes in respect of the form of constitution which they reveal.

Class I. Those which mention a king, a prostates[1] of the Molossians and a secretary, and record decisions of the "koinon" or "ecclesia" of the Molossians. Collitz, 1334, 1335, 1337.[2]

Class II. Those which mention a prostates without reference to a king or secretary, and record decisions of "the Molossians".[3] Collitz, 1340–41.

Class III. One inscription which mentions a king and prostates, but no secretary, and is a decision of the "symmachoi of the Epirots". Collitz, 1336.

All the examples of class I come from the reign of a King Alexander, i.e. either from between 343 and 330 or from between 272 and about 240. The king of the one inscription of class III is that Neoptolemus, son of Alexander, whose identity we have discussed in Appendix III and whose reign, in any event, must fall somewhere between 330 and 297. It is, therefore, certain that an "alliance of the Epirots" existed at some moment between these years, and it is among the chief tasks of those who deal with Epirot inscriptions[4] to determine what is the relation—temporal and constitutional—between this body and the "koinon" or

---

[1] See p. 18 n. 2.

[2] With the readings of 1335 and 1337 given by Nilsson, pp. 59–93.

[3] Although the inscriptions of class II do not mention a king, their general style and the absence of any reference in them to the "koinon" and "strategos" of the Epirots, which we know to have taken the place of the monarchy, make it probable that they are earlier than the setting up of a republic. But see Busolt, p. 1474 n. 5.

[4] E.g. Nilsson; Busolt, pp. 1470–77; Swoboda in Hermann's *Lehrbuch*; Beloch, III. 2. 177; Kaerst's article "Epirus" in Pauly-Wissowa; Klotzsch; Schubert; and Tarn, *Antigonos Gonatas*, p. 55.

"ecclesia" of the Molossians mentioned in the inscriptions of class I.

Nilsson, noticing that various persons appear as "pro-statai" of the Molossians in inscriptions of class I who seem to have come from parts of Epirus outside Molossia itself, drew the conclusion that the "koinon" of the Molossians was an organisa-tion embracing the whole of Epirus which had grown up under the hegemony of the Molossians and their royal house in the course of the fourth century, existed under King Alexander I, and was replaced during the reign of his son[1] by an "alliance of the Epirots"—a delegate assembly in which the predominance of the Molossians was less marked, and which endured until the end of the monarchy, when its place was taken by the "koinon" of the Epirots.[2] To Beloch, however, this account of Epirot con-stitutional development appears "grotesque". For his part he insists that the "koinon" or "ecclesia" of the Molossians which we find in the inscriptions was confined to Molossia proper, that there were also "koina" of the other Epirot tribes of which we cannot expect to hear anything in a series of inscriptions coming exclusively from the Molossian capital, and that all these tribal "koina" co-existed with and sent deputies to the "symmachy" of the Epirots.[3]

It is, I think, the case that neither of these theories can be accepted in its entirety. The first, as Beloch has pointed out, is directly opposed to all analogy. For while commonly a loose tribal alliance gives way to the closer union of the "koinon", Nilsson and the rest reverse this process and make the "koinon" disappear in favour of a looser organisation. But—more than this—it is of the essence of their theory that the Alexander of the inscriptions is King Alexander I, and that the constitution re-vealed by them—the "koinon" with its various officers, and its combination of monarchy and republic—existed in Epirus for some time before 330. If this is so, it follows that the semi-barbarian Epirots were politically in advance of their Greek neighbours in Aetolia; for the "koinon" of the Aetolians—as

[1] Nilsson is one of those who hold that Neoptolemus was a son of Alexander I.

[2] This view is accepted in its essentials by Busolt, Swoboda and Tarn.

[3] Beloch is supported by Klotzsch.

distinguished from a confederacy of the various Aetolian tribes—first appears in 314, while its coins and inscriptions date from after the Gallic invasion of 280.[1] Yet the Aetolians are generally credited with being the originators of developed federalism in North-West Greece, and it is inherently far more probable that the Epirots should have imitated them than that they should have imitated the Epirots.[2]

Beloch's own theory, on the other hand, though it is not necessarily open to the criticism that it dates the Alexander inscriptions in the fourth century,[3] has its own weakness in its failure to dispose of the evidence which Nilsson has collected to show that non-Molossians were sometimes elected "prostatai" of the Molossians. One example will, perhaps, suffice. Inscription 1351 contains two lists of witnesses to a grant of freedom to a slave, one of Molossians and one of Thesprotians; among the Thesprotian witnesses is a man who is described as from "Onopernos" and the whole inscription is dated "ἐπὶ προστάτα Φιλοξένου Ὀνοπέρνου". If it is objected that Philoxenus was not prostates of the Molossians but only some temple official at Dodona, we have only to turn to inscription 1346 to read "προστατεύοντος Σαβύρωνος Μολοσσῶν Ὀνοπέρνου Καρτατοῦ". Beloch, of course, is ready with an answer to this too—"aber wer sagt uns denn dass nicht ein Teil der Onoperner, eben die Kartatoi, den Molossern gehört hat?"—but it is not a convincing answer.

Further, it is a weakness common to both theories that they take no account of the inscriptions of class II as a type independent of class I, although the differences between the two are hardly to be explained as due entirely to that inaccuracy which it is natural to find in early examples of recording in any country.[4]

---

[1] For the development of the Aetolian league see Busolt, p. 1509; Diodorus, XIX. 66. 2.

[2] Nilsson himself remarks (p. 65) that the fully developed "Kanzleistil" first appears in Epirus in inscriptions of the Republic (e.g. 1339, c. 175) and seems to have been imitated from Aetolia.

[3] Beloch himself seems to accept the early dating, but if the "koinon" was, as he thinks, a purely Molossian assembly which need not be brought into any temporal relation with the symmachy of c. 300, we are free to date its inscriptions in the third century.

[4] Nilsson (p. 60) dates inscription 1340 in the reign of Alexander I (i.e. making it contemporary with class I). Beloch does not mention his date for it.

The occurrence in the inscriptions of class II of "Molossians" instead of "the koinon of the Molossians" would of itself prove nothing, and the absence of the secretary perhaps not much; but how is the absence of the name of the king of Molossia from a Molossian inscription to be explained except on the assumption that the inscription dates from a time when there was no king? The Molossian monarchy was certainly a kingship with limited powers, but not more limited than those of the kings of Sparta who appear on inscriptions beside the ephors, and it must be remembered that it is "Alcetas" and "Neoptolemus", and not the "Molossians", who are allies of Athens in her second confederacy.[1]

It may, then, be conjectured that the inscriptions of class II are to be dated in an interval of republicanism among the Molossians, and if we except the period after the final fall of the royal house,[2] we know of only two such intervals: one in the years immediately after 264, when Alexander II lost his crown for a time as a result of his unsuccessful intervention in the Chremonidean War, and the other—if we accept the conclusions reached in Appendix III—between 317 and 312. Between these two our choice would be difficult if we had not internal evidence to help us, but it happens that one of these inscriptions (1340) refers to the presence of envoys from Acragas at Dodona, and it happens, too, that we know both that Acragas was sacked in 261 and that Acragantine envoys were sailing up the west coast of Greece in 314. It would, therefore, be better to choose the earlier date.[3]

Now to summarise the results to which we seem to have attained. Neither of the current theories as to the arrangement and inter-

---

[1] Cf. p. 34 above.

[2] Busolt dates the inscriptions of class II after 235 and it would be better to follow him than to make them contemporary with those of class I, but on the assumption (for which see p. 109 n. 3) that they are of an earlier date one must look for republican intervals in the period of the monarchy.

[3] Sack of Acragas, Polybius, I. 17–19; Diodorus, XXIII. 11–14; Zonaras, VIII. 10. In 314 the city was the headquarters of the Sicilian oligarchs who were fighting against Agathocles. The envoys had been sent to bring Prince Acrotatus of Sparta to Sicily, and touched at Apollonia on their return journey: Diodorus, XIX. 70. 4. It is tempting to bring them into connection with inscription 1340, but the conjecture is clearly not one on which much reliance can be placed.

pretation of the Dodona inscriptions can be accepted. Those which have been called class I are to be placed with some confidence in the reign of Alexander II, and are the records of an organisation which extended beyond the limits of Molossia itself. Those of class II, on the other hand, can hardly be contemporary with these, may be the record of a purely Molossian assembly and can be dated without much confidence in the later years of the fourth century. The inscription of class III—mentioning the "symmachy of the Epirots"—is to be dated between 330 and 297.

I have alluded to these results from time to time in the text, but it will, perhaps, be useful to give here a brief summary of the whole course of constitutional development which they suggest.

At the time of the Peloponnesian War there was no "Epirot" organisation. Each tribe had its own assembly presided over by annually elected magistrates: e.g. the "prostates" of the Molossians. The Molossians were the only tribe which had preserved their monarchy. It is extremely unlikely that any records of proceedings were made at this time (chapter I).

In the course of the fourth century the Molossians under their kings established a sort of suzerainty over the other tribes which was given a constitutional dress about 330 in the form of the "symmachy of the Epirots", comprising a delegate assembly presided over by the "prostates" of the Molossians, and a "hegemon" in the person of the Molossian king. The individual tribal assemblies went on exactly as before, and it is possible that they followed the example of the delegate assembly in keeping "records". We have slight evidence that the Molossian tribal assembly did so about 314, but the circumstances may have been exceptional (chapter II).

Both delegate and tribal assemblies probably continued as before during the reign of Pyrrhus, but it is likely that their powers were in fact very slight. Pyrrhus strove to change the monarchy from a Molossian kingship to an Epirot kingship and in general to make a united state of Epirus (chapter III).

About 263 the "symmachy" was broken up by King Antigonus of Macedon, who did not desire a united Epirus. The separate tribal assemblies continued and, no doubt, became more highly organised under the influence of the example of the Aetolians. Then King Alexander II, who had been driven into exile by Antigonus, regained his Molossian crown, and a re-union of Epirus came about by sympolity with the Molossians, i.e. other tribal "koina" were amalgamated with the Molossian "koinon". Then (about 232) the monarchy was abolished and the Molossian "koinon" gave place to an Epirot "koinon" with an annually elected "strategos". The change from "Molossian" to "Epirot" is probably to be explained as due to a decline in the importance of the Molossians on the final disappearance of the kingship, which was itself essentially Molossian (chapter IV).

APPENDIX V

I THE NEGOTIATIONS FOR A PEACE BETWEEN PYRRHUS AND ROME

THERE is considerable difference of opinion among historians as to the time and place of the peace negotiations between Pyrrhus and the Roman senate. One view is that Cineas was sent to Rome after the battle of Heraclea, and that his visit was the occasion of the one and only attempt to make peace.[1] Another—and more popular—view is that Cineas went to Rome after Asculum and not after Heraclea.[2] A third view is that Cineas went twice to Rome, once after Heraclea and again after Asculum.[3] My own view is that he went only once to Rome—after Heraclea—but that in the early part of 278 there was another attempt to make peace, and that on this occasion the negotiations were conducted in Campania.

The authorities are:

(i) Plutarch, *Pyrrhus*, 18. Cineas sent to Rome during Pyrrhus' march on the city. The terms which he offers are rejected. Ch. 20: A Roman embassy comes to Tarentum at the end of 280 to treat for a return of the prisoners taken at Heraclea. Pyrrhus releases them on parole: they are to come back if the senate refuses to ratify the peace. (This is, of course, in direct contradiction to ch. 18, in which the senate has already rejected Cineas' terms. Plutarch has combined two incompatible versions.) Ch. 21: Pyrrhus makes a second attempt at a peace when Fabricius is consul, i.e. in 278.

(ii) Livy (*Epitome*, XIII) mentions only one visit of Cineas to Rome. It took place before the battle of Asculum, but after Fabricius had come to Tarentum to negotiate about the prisoners. (It is, of course, possible that in the full text there was mention of a second visit of Cineas to Rome.)

(iii) Eutropius (dependent on Livy) mentions Fabricius' embassy to Tarentum and then that of Cineas to Rome, but says nothing of a second visit.

---

[1] This is the view of Schubert and von Scala.

[2] This view was first put forward by Niese (*Hermes*, 1896) and has been accepted by Beloch (IV. 1. 551 n. 1).

[3] Cf. Judeich, *Klio* (1926).

(iv) Justin (XVIII. 1–2) mentions Cineas' journey to Rome to obtain the ratification of a treaty which he had made with Fabricius. (Niese and Beloch consider that Justin dated this visit in the spring of 278, but see below.)

(v) Appian, *Samnitica*, 10, speaks of an embassy of Cineas immediately after the battle of Heraclea and then of Fabricius' mission to Tarentum. He betrays the same confusion as Plutarch, for he, too, speaks of prisoners being sent back on parole as though the peace terms had not—on his own showing—been already rejected. He records a second visit of Cineas to Rome after Asculum.

(vi) Dionysius (XIX. 17. 20) implies that Pyrrhus began his negotiations with Rome before Fabricius came to Tarentum.

(vii) Dion and Zonaras (frg. 40. 26). Fabricius comes to Pyrrhus, and then Cineas goes to Rome. Zonaras mentions a second attempt at peace after the battle of Asculum, but does not speak of a second visit of Cineas to Rome.

The first point to be noted is that the tradition preserved by Plutarch, Appian and Dionysius that Cineas came to Rome before Fabricius went to Tarentum is inconsistent with what they themselves relate of the negotiations at Tarentum, and is easily to be explained as a fiction of Roman pride: Pyrrhus, not Rome, was the first to think of peace. It is, therefore, to be neglected.[1] Next it is to be noticed that all the authorities—with the possible exception of Justin—speak of a mission of Fabricius to Tarentum after the battle of Heraclea, and that the story, preserved by Plutarch and Appian, that some of the prisoners were allowed to return to celebrate the Saturnalia at Rome, implies that the embassy came to Pyrrhus in the late autumn or early winter. Beloch and Niese reject this embassy of 280 altogether and place Fabricius' visit to Tarentum in the spring of 278, that is to say,

---

[1] Judeich (*Klio*, 1926) disagrees and puts forward the far-fetched argument apparently accepted in *C.A.H.* (VII. p. 646) that Cineas' behaviour in Rome showed an ignorance of the Romans which would have been impossible if he had already met Fabricius. But there were plenty of Tarentines from whom he could have learnt something, not to speak of the many Roman prisoners, and I see no reason why the addition of Fabricius to these would have induced him to desert the ordinary methods of hellenistic diplomacy in which he had been trained.

they consider that the Saturnalia story is worthless and that Justin is better evidence than all the rest together.

Now it is true that Justin is chiefly derived from Greek sources, but it is also true that the Roman annalists, from whom our other authorities descend, often depended themselves on Greek sources and it is most uncritical to regard them as worthless when—as in this case—their version of events is no more creditable to the Romans than that which it is sought to prefer to it. Furthermore, it must be remembered that Justin is an epitome of an epitome, and although, at first sight, it certainly appears that he dates Fabricius' visit to Tarentum in the spring of 278, a closer examination tends to dispel this impression. In bk XVIII, chs. 1–2, he begins by recounting Pyrrhus' warfare in Italy. First he describes the battle of Heraclea—in terms which, incidentally, point to a Roman rather than a Greek source—and says that Pyrrhus was wounded in it, which is a confusion with the battle of Asculum. He then goes on to describe that battle— which was fought a year after Heraclea in the following terms: "interjectis diebus cum sociorum exercitus supervenisset iterato proelium cum Romanis facit". The supporters of his chronological accuracy are here forced to assert that with him "interjectis diebus" does not mean "a few days later" but "some time later", i.e. here "next year". The example (bk XXII. 8. 7) which is adduced to support this statement is not very fortunate, for in it the second event follows the first at an interval of a few weeks. The fact is, of course, that Justin did not worry whether Asculum was fought in the same year as Heraclea or not. He assumed that it was, and just said "afterwards"; if he had been clear as to the twelve months' interval, he would never have used such an expression. Next he describes Mago's activities and introduces them with the word "interea" as though they were coincident with the battle of Asculum, whereas in reality they fall quite six months later. Then he describes Fabricius' visit to Tarentum and Cineas' visit to Rome, and joins them on to Mago's activities with the words "dum haec aguntur". Niese and Beloch insist that these words are proof that Cineas' visit was in the spring of 278—for that is undoubtedly the date of Mago's arrival—but why should we take "dum haec aguntur" more seriously than we took "interjectis diebus" or "interea"? Is it not clear that Justin recorded separately first the warfare, then the Carthaginian intervention, and then the negotiations, and tacked them all together without any regard for chronology? I believe, in fact, that Justin is no evidence against Cineas' visit to Rome in November 280, because it is just this visit that he describes.

But although I cannot agree with Niese and Beloch in eliminating Fabricius' visit to Tarentum and Cineas' visit to Rome from the history of the year 280, still less can I agree with Schubert and von Scala in thinking that these negotiations in 280 were the only negotiations, or with Judeich and the *Cambridge Ancient History* in making Cineas come to Rome again in 278. It is clear that there were negotiations in 278—negotiations that Mago was sent to wreck—and it seems probable that they were conducted in Campania.

Those of our authorities that mention the place of the negotiations which they record at the end of 280 agree in putting them at Tarentum, but the negotiations of 278 they bring into connection with the celebrated—if apocryphal—story that Fabricius—when consul in 278 and facing Pyrrhus in the field—rejected an offer of the royal physician to poison his master.[1] If there had been a campaign in 278, it would probably have been waged in Campania,[2] and so it is plausible to suppose that the negotiations in the field took place there. This opinion receives a little confirmation from Justin's statement that Mago visited Pyrrhus in an interval of his own negotiations with the senate in 278. It would have been easy enough for him to coast down to Gaeta or Naples, but Beloch is forced to assume that he sailed round to Tarentum. As to the theory that Cineas came twice to Rome, I agree with Beloch in suspecting that one visit is a double of the other, but whereas he holds that

---

[1] These differences in the circumstances of the two sets of negotiations as recorded by our authorities tell against Beloch's view that they are doubled like Cineas' two visits to Rome. He chooses to throw over the negotiations in the field between Fabricius as consul and Pyrrhus, and to bring Fabricius to Tarentum in the early spring of 278 as "legatus" before entering on his consulate.

[2] Part at least of Pyrrhus' army seems to have wintered in Campania in 280 to 279 (Appian, *Samnitica*, 10. 2; Eutropius, II. 12) and if—as is likely—he cleared Apulia in the campaign of 279, he would be preparing for an attack on the strongly defended Liris valley in 278.

the visit of 280 is fictitious, although practically all our authorities refer to it, I would see a fiction in the visit of 278 which has so little support from them.

II THE TERMS PROPOSED

Our authorities for the terms which Pyrrhus offered to the senate are:

(i) Appian (*Samnitica*, 10). Peace, friendship and alliance for Rome, Pyrrhus and the Tarentines. Freedom and autonomy for the other Greeks and the return of all territory conquered from the Lucanians and Samnites.

(ii) "Ineditum Vaticanum" (published by von Arnim in *Hermes*, 1892, p. 120). Rome to confine herself to Latium.

(iii) Eutropius, II. 12. 4. Pyrrhus to keep what he had at the time.

(iv) Plutarch, ch. 18. In return for immunity for Tarentum Pyrrhus will help Rome to subdue Italy.

These are all recorded as offers made at the first negotiations in 280; (i), (ii) and (iii) are in substantial agreement for Samnium and Lucania had joined Pyrrhus; I imagine that the point on which negotiations broke down was Campania, for although Pyrrhus had apparently quartered some of his forces there for the winter of 280–79 it might be doubted whether he was in effective possession of it; (iv) is, of course, absurd and is contradicted by Plutarch himself when he makes Appius Claudius say that the Samnites will laugh at the Romans if they accept such terms. It is difficult to say how much farther Pyrrhus went in his endeavour to make peace in 278. Probably he abandoned his claim to Campania, but not the independence of the Samnites and Lucanians.[1]

III THE SITUATION OF THE ITALIOT GREEKS DURING PYRRHUS' SICILIAN EXPEDITION

It is commonly said that the Greeks in Italy were hard pressed by the Romans during Pyrrhus' absence in Sicily. If we were right in saying that he took only 9000 men with him—see note 1 to page 77—then there were at least 10,000 left in Italy, and, in fact,

---

[1] Judeich believes that Plutarch gives the terms which Pyrrhus offered in 278: but it seems to me incredible that at that time he was ready to throw over his Italian allies and all Greek Italy except Tarentum.

Justin, XVIII. 2. 12, expressly says that strong garrisons were put in the chief towns. It would, therefore, be very surprising if the Romans were able to conduct operations against the Italiots at all, and the fact that Pyrrhus had to go so far north as Beneventum to find them in 275 seems to indicate a very different state of affairs from that which prevailed in 280 when Laevinus attacked him at Heraclea. Nor do the individual texts, on which the Roman successes against the Italiots in these years depend, bear a close examination. The revolt of Locri recorded in Appian, *Samnitica* 11 and the winning over of Heraclea by Fabricius in 278 mentioned by Cicero (*Pro Balbo*, 22) are disposed of by Beloch in IV. 1. 555 n. 2 and 642 n. 1 respectively. Nor does the capture of Croton by the Consul Rufinus in 277, recorded by Zonaras (VIII. 6) and Frontinus (*Strat.* III. 6. 4), appear to me any more credible. According to it Croton and Locri were without Greek garrisons at the time of the consul's approach and appealed for help to Milo in Tarentum. Nicomachus, who was sent across with a small force to guard them, lost Croton through a trick of Rufinus', but succeeded in holding Locri. Suddenly, however, although a Roman army was in the neighbourhood, he returned to Tarentum, which was in no need of defence, and abandoned Locri, which was invaluable as a port as long as Pyrrhus was in Sicily. Is it not clear that all this took place after Pyrrhus' return to Greece, when the only Epirot force left was Milo's garrison in Tarentum, and that Nicomachus abandoned Locri in 271 when they were all ordered back to Epirus? If this is so, it was not the consul Rufinus who captured Croton, and, as a matter of fact, it was probably no consul at all, but the Campanians of Rhegion; for the Romans would hardly have treated the city in the way described in Livy, XXIV. 3.

IV THE ARMY WITH WHICH PYRRHUS INVADED MACEDON IN 274

In addition to the 8500 troops brought from Italy there would naturally be a certain number of men in Epirus who had been left to garrison the country or had grown up between 280 and 275—though, in this connection, one must remember that Pyrrhus must have been reinforced from time to time during his Western expedition.

From Plutarch—*Pyrrhus*, 26—it appears that some Gauls were engaged, but even so the army cannot well have exceeded 15,000, and its success—as Plutarch's account shows—was due in the main to the bad spirit of the Macedonians. Tarn (*Antigonos Gonatas*, p. 263 and App. 7, and *C.A.H.* VII. 213), not content with this explanation, thinks that Pyrrhus had a large army, and has to account for its existence by postulating a subsidy from Ptolemy Philadelphus and Arsinoe, which enabled the Epirot king to hire troops, e.g. Gauls, Aetolians, Acarnanians, etc. on a large scale. If this hypothesis is to be accepted we must be sure (*a*) that Ptolemy was an enemy of Antigonus in 275 and desired his expulsion from Macedon, (*b*) that he was a friend of Pyrrhus. As to (*a*), apart from this suggestion of Tarn's there is no trace of Egyptian opposition to Antigonus between 286 and 270. It is no doubt true that an established power in Macedon was bound in the long run to come into conflict with the Ptolemies, but Antigonus' position before 271 was not such as would justify Philadelphus in making an enemy of him at a time when he was himself at war with Antiochus. Further, the scholiast on Callimachus, *Hymn to Delos*, 175, seems to me evidence that the kings of Macedon and Egypt were friends about 275. It says that at about that time Ptolemy obtained a force of Gallic mercenaries from "a certain Antigonus who was his friend", and since Gonatas certainly had a number of Gauls to spare after 276, many scholars believe that he is the Antigonus meant. Against this Tarn argues—quite reasonably—that "a certain Antigonus" is an odd way of referring to a famous king, and that "Antigonus" was an Egyptian recruiting agent and one of Ptolemy's "φίλοι" (the scholiast writing "φίλος ὤν" instead of "τῶν φίλων"). But I do not think that one could possibly describe the procuring of Gauls by such a man—a servant of Ptolemy— with the word "προξενεῖν", which implies an independent position. Therefore, even if one does not accept Wachsmuth's emendation of "Τινος" to "Γονατου", there seems a balance in favour of identifying the Antigonus of the scholiast with the king of Macedon. As to (*b*), it is established that Ptolemy sent a friendly embassy to Rome in 273. Tarn remarks that this "does not import hostility to Pyrrhus". Of course it does not, but it is hardly consistent with the friendship which should have existed between them if Philadelphus financed the invasion of Macedon.

APPENDIX VI

THE DATE OF THE DEATH OF KING
ACROTATUS OF SPARTA

AT first sight this question may seem to have little connection with Epirot history, but indirectly it has a considerable bearing upon the question of the date of the invasion of Macedon by King Alexander. In itself it is likely enough that this invasion should have taken place—as Justin (XXVI. 2. 9) says that it did—before the end of the Chremonidean War, and if it is to be given a later date it is really essential to make it coincide with an attack on Antigonus from some other quarter, for it is inconceivable that the king of a much weakened Epirus should have been rash enough to attack the king of Macedon after his complete victory over Athens and Sparta alone and unaided. Beloch thinks that the invasion can be made to coincide with the campaign which ended with the defeat and death of King Acrotatus at the battle of Megalopolis, which he seems to date about 258.[1] It is the purpose of this Appendix to show that this battle must have been fought at latest in 262, and so to deprive Beloch's date for Alexander's invasion of Macedon of an essential foundation. It is admitted that a "terminus post quem" for the death of Acrotatus is the battle of Corinth in which his father Areus lost his life and which is to be dated either in 265 or 264,[2] and that a "terminus ante quem" of about 253 is afforded by the fact that Leonidas was the Agiad king of Sparta in 244 and that between him and Acrotatus time must be allowed for the eight years' reign of Acrotatus' son, the boy king Areus II.[3]

We know that in 241 Chilonis, daughter of King Leonidas, was a married woman with two children, one of whom was old enough to walk, and that her brother Cleomenes—"although not quite of a proper age for marriage"—was in fact given a wife in that year.[4] From this it follows that the marriage of Leonidas with Cratesiclea, the mother of Chilonis and Cleomenes, can

---

[1] Plutarch, *Agis*, 3; Pausanias, VIII. 27. 11; Beloch, IV. 1. 597.
[2] Diodorus, XX. 29. 1; Trogus, *Prologue*, 26.
[3] Plutarch, *Agis*, 3; Pausanias, III. 6. 6.
[4] Plutarch, *Agis*, 17–18; Cleomenes, 1.

hardly be put later than 259.[1] This was not, however, Leonidas' first marriage, for he had gone out to Syria as a settler (ἐπὶ μετοικισμῷ) in the days of Seleucus Nicator (i.e. before 280) and had there married a native woman by whom he had children.[2] What induced him to abandon his establishment abroad and return to Sparta to marry Cratesiclea? If one considers that his father Cleonymus had been a mortal enemy of both Areus and Acrotatus,[3] one may think that it is very unlikely that he returned in Acrotatus' lifetime, and that it was in fact the news of his death which brought him home, since he then became head of the Agiad house, regent, if the queen, who was pregnant, bore a son, and king of Sparta himself, if she did not.

If this is so, one must allow time between the death of Acrotatus and the marriage of Leonidas with Cratesiclea for the news to reach Syria, for Leonidas to wind up his affairs there, return to Greece and choose a wife. It is not, I think, too much to say that 260, if not 261, is—from this point of view—the last possible year for the battle of Megalopolis. But if once we come to the conclusion that Acrotatus' death must be placed as early as this, then we must place it earlier still. In the autumn of 262 Athens capitulated and the long struggle of the Chremonidean War ended in the triumph of Antigonus Gonatas. Is it in the least degree probable that Sparta would have chosen 261 or 260 for a renewed attack; and is it not very probable that it was in the hope of creating a diversion that might lead to the raising of the siege that Acrotatus led out the Spartan army once more despite the losses suffered so recently in the battle of Corinth? The battle of Megalopolis is, therefore, to be placed in 263 or 262, and the birth of King Areus II and the return of Leonidas in 262 or 261.

[1] Beloch, in fact, puts Cleomenes' birth about 260 (IV. 2. 162).
[2] Plutarch, *Agis*, 3 and 11.
[3] Plutarch. *Pyrrhus*. 26.

APPENDIX VII

KING ALEXANDER II AND THE LATER
AEACIDS

BELOCH places the death of King Alexander II "about 255", and supports this date with an elaborate chain of reasoning.[1] Tarn and Holleaux, in the *Cambridge Ancient History*, say "about 240", but they give no reasons for their decision and counter Beloch's arguments with a genealogical device which cannot be justified.[2] Nevertheless, I believe that 240 is, in fact, more nearly right than 255.

It is characteristic of the condition of our chronology in the middle of the third century that the fixed point from which one must start is so remote as the death of Hieron of Syracuse, which is to be placed either in 215 or 214.[3] His grandson and heir, Hieronymus, was fifteen years old at the time and it seems that his granddaughter, Harmonia, was a little older.[4] Therefore the marriage of their parents, the prince Gelon of Syracuse and the Epirot princess Nereis, can hardly be later than 232, or Nereis' birth, in its turn, much later than 250. Our first difficulty is to fit her and her sister Deidameia[5] into the Aeacid family tree.

All the authorities who mention the father of these princesses agree that he was a Pyrrhus, and one must resist the temptation to simplify matters by following Droysen, Niese and the *Cambridge Ancient History* in calling them daughters of King Alexander.[6] They can hardly have been daughters of the great

[1] Beloch, IV. 2. 150.

[2] *C.A.H.* VII. 733 and 828, and the genealogical tables at the end of the volume in which Nereis and Deidameia are made daughters of Alexander in defiance of all the evidence.

[3] Beloch says 214; Niese, 215. No other year is possible.

[4] Livy, XXIV. 4 and 24–5.

[5] Justin, XXVIII. 3, calls her Laodamia, but there is no doubt that she is the same woman as the Deidameia of Polyaenus, VIII. 52, and Pausanias, IV. 35. 3.

[6] Polyaenus and Pausanias (*ubi supra*), Polybius, VII. 4. 5, and Pausanias, VI. 12. 3, all say that her father was Pyrrhus. The two latter passages speak of Pyrrhus I, but Pausanias, IV. 35. 3, says Pyrrhus II, and it is clear that the better known figure could easily be substituted for the less familiar.

Pyrrhus, for he died in 272, so that even if one assumed that they were born in his last years and long after his other children, Nereis would have been forty when she married—an unexampled age for the first marriage of a hellenistic princess.[1] Unless, therefore, one is prepared to invent an otherwise unknown member of the royal house, the father of Nereis and Deidameia was Pyrrhus II, the grandson of Pyrrhus I. Modern historians have followed Justin in calling him a son of King Alexander. For myself I prefer to follow Pausanias in making him a son of Alexander's elder brother Ptolemaeus; but for the moment it is only important to notice that the father of a daughter born at latest about 250 cannot have been born himself much after 270.[2]

The next difficulty is to combine this result with what evidence there is for the history of the last years of the monarchy in Epirus. The chief account is given by Justin,[3] who says that on Alexander's death his widow, Olympias, became regent for his two sons Pyrrhus and Ptolemaeus; that during her regency she married her daughter Phthia to Demetrius II of Macedon; that the two princes succeeded to the throne in turn and both died without issue, and that the royal house was thus reduced to two princesses, one of whom married Gelon of Syracuse, while the other was murdered by the Epirots. At first sight this account provides us with a "terminus ante quem" for the death of Alexander II, for if Pyrrhus was born at latest about 270 he could not need a regent unless he succeeded to the throne by about 255.[4] But quite apart from the fact that the marriage of Phthia with Demetrius is now known to have taken place after 245,[5] a date "about 255" for the death of Alexander is inconsistent with the evidence of Trogus and of Polyaenus.

Trogus[6] included the death of Alexander and the events which followed upon it in Epirus in his twenty-eighth book. In his twenty-sixth book he had brought the history of Greece down to

---

[1] There is no reason to suppose that Nereis was a widow—indeed Justin calls her "virgo"—so her case cannot be compared with that of Berenice or Nicaea of Corinth.

[2] Justin, XXVIII. 1 and 3; Pausanias, IV. 35. 3.

[3] *Ubi supra.*

[4] Sixteen was about the age for personal rule. Cf. Livy, XXIV. 4. 9.

[5] Tarn, *Classical Quarterly*, XVIII. 17.

[6] Trogus, *Prologues.*

Aratus' capture of Corinth (243) and the history of Asia down to the death of Antiochus Theos (246). Book twenty-seven continued the history of Asia down to about 228 and Trogus took up Greek affairs again in book twenty-eight. It is natural to suppose that he took them up where he left them.

Polyaenus[1] says that during the revolution which led to the fall of the monarchy in Epirus the mob at Ambracia sent one of Alexander's gentleman-at-arms ($\tau\hat{\omega}\nu$ Ἀλεξάνδρου σωματοφυλάκων) to kill the princess Deidameia. This murder cannot be dated before 235, and yet if Alexander is King Alexander II—and who else can he be?—it is not probable that the man would be described as one of his "somatophylaces" unless his death had been fairly recent.[2]

There is, then, fairly good evidence to show that "about 240" is a "terminus post quem"[3] for the death of Alexander II, and from this it follows that Justin is wrong in saying that Pyrrhus II was a child at the time; but he is not very likely to have been wrong as to the fact of a regency of Olympias, and one may conjecture that she was regent for Ptolemaeus only. If her regency began—as Justin says it did—on Alexander's death, Pyrrhus must have predeceased him and the statement of Syncellus, which has troubled historians, to the effect that the last six kings of Epirus reigned for ninety years seems to confirm this conclusion. The monarchy fell about 232, and reckoning from the Lamian War (322) we have as kings in Epirus Aeacides, Alcetas II, Neoptolemus II, Pyrrhus, Alexander II and Ptolemaeus, whom Polyaenus shows to have been the last Aeacid.[4] Ovid preserves a story that the younger Pyrrhus was poisoned by Olympias, and it may well be that his death, occurring just before that of Alex-

[1] VIII. 52.

[2] The marriage of Gelon and Nereis must have preceded the fall of the monarchy in Epirus, and that marriage, in view of the fact that there seem to have been no children of it older than Harmonia and Hieronymus, can hardly have taken place before 235.

[3] Since the marriage of Demetrius II and Phthia must come before 238 when the issue of it—King Philip V—was born, and Justin states that this marriage was arranged by Olympias after Alexander's death, we seem to have a "terminus ante quem" for that event. But it is not safe to rely on Justin's chronology.

[4] Syncellus, 578. Cf. p. 108 above.

ander II and assuring the old queen of the control of affairs, gave rise to the rumour.[1]

Our third and last difficulty concerns the parentage of Pyrrhus the younger and Ptolemaeus whom Justin asserts to have been brothers and sons of Alexander II and Olympias. Pyrrhus—as we have seen—was born at latest about 270. It is, of course, quite possible that he was a son of Alexander (born *c.* 295) but Pausanias preserves a genealogy which makes him the son of Ptolemaeus, the eldest son of Pyrrhus I, who was killed in 272 a few weeks before his father. Pausanias' authority seems to me preferable to that of Justin, and it is easy to imagine that in the crisis of 272 Alexander was declared king in place of his baby nephew and that he subsequently adopted him as his son.[2] In this connection it is perhaps worth noticing that it is more plausible to suppose that Olympias poisoned her nephew than her own son. As to Ptolemaeus—he was in need of a regent about 240 and therefore belongs to the same generation as the princesses Nereis and Deidameia (born about 250). It is possible that he was—as Justin says—a son of Alexander and a brother of Phthia, but his name inclines me to believe that he was a son of the younger Pyrrhus and named after his grandfather, and a brother of Nereis and her sister.[3]

In conclusion it may be noted that the various authorities for the family history of the Aeacids after the death of Pyrrhus I cannot by any means be all of them reconciled, and that while the suggestions here put forward only reject the evidence of Justin, the theory suggested in the *Cambridge Ancient History* involves the rejection of Polybius, Polyaenus and Pausanias (twice) while Beloch's view is inconsistent with Polyaenus and Trogus as well as Justin.

[1] *Ibis*, 307, where "dictus modo rex" is Pyrrhus I.

[2] Pausanias, IV. 35. 3, where Ptolemaeus, the father of Pyrrhus II, is, of course, the elder brother of Alexander, and not—as stated—his son. One may compare the accession of Antigonus Doson to the throne of Macedon and his adoption of the boy prince Philip.

[3] One may also note that if Olympias was a daughter of Antigone (see Beloch, IV. 2. 148) she was born at latest about 294 and is not likely to have had a son who needed a regent in 239.

APPENDIX VIII

EPIRUS AND ACARNANIA

THE relations between the peoples of Acarnania and Aetolia and the kingdoms of Epirus and Macedon in the third century B.C. have long been a subject of controversy between historians and have lately been re-examined by Dr Klaffenbach,[1] who, as a result of a detailed discussion of the views of his precursors, arrives at new conclusions of his own. For myself I doubt whether the evidence at our disposal is as yet sufficient to warrant a confident decision in favour of any of the many alternatives at our disposal, but I must at least attempt to justify the choices which I have made in the text. The dispute centres on the dates and the circumstances surrounding four events—(a) the Aetolo-Acarnanian treaty discovered at Thermum,[2] (b) the expulsion of King Alexander II of Epirus from his kingdom, (c) his restoration,[3] (d) the partition of Acarnania between Alexander and the Aetolians[4]—but for a proper consideration of these questions it is, in my opinion, necessary to go back some fifty years farther into the past and trace the relations of the several states from the Lamian War.

Of all the confederate Greeks the Aetolians had been the least broken by the Macedonian power. From their mountain retreats they bade a fairly effective defiance to Antipater and to his son Cassander after him, and offered the best field of operations to the agents whom Antigonus sent over from Asia to stir up trouble for the rulers of Macedon. To the westward of the Aetolians, between the river Achelous and the sea, dwelt a smaller and more civilised people—the Acarnanians—who dreaded nothing more than to be swallowed up by their powerful neighbours. To support and strengthen the weaker state against his enemies

[1] "Die Zeit des Ätolisch-Akarnanischen Bundesvertrages", *Klio*, XXIV. (1931), 223–34.

[2] First published in 1905. Klaffenbach (p. 223) mentions the most important contributions made towards its elucidation. It is *Syll.*[3] 421.

[3] Our one authority for (b) and (c) is Justin, XXVI. 2. 9 and 3. 1.

[4] Polybius, II. 45. 1; IX. 34. 7; Justin, XXVI. 3. 1; XXVIII. 1. 1.

in Aetolia was an obvious policy for Cassander to pursue and in 314 we find him engaged upon it.[1] At that time the influence of Macedon in North-West Greece was at its height. King Aeacides of Molossia had been expelled from his kingdom some three years before and Epirus was now organised as a republic under the surveillance of Cassander's "epimelete" Lyciscus.[2] Further to the north Atintania was Macedonian[3] and in this very year Cassander was to gain control of Apollonia and Epidamnus, and to defeat the Illyrian Glaucias.[4] To the south of Epirus Ambracia was probably garrisoned by Macedonian troops,[5] while in this year again the king of Macedon was to gain a short-lived control over Leucas.[6] It is fairly clear too, though nowhere, I think, explicitly stated, that the peoples such as the Athamanians and Amphilochians[7] who formed a bridge to the north-west of Aetolia between the southern frontier of Cassander's kingdom of Thessaly and the Acarnanians must also have been controlled by him. It is unfortunate that we do not know more of the relation in which these various cities and peoples stood to Macedon. It is obvious, of course, that they were not considered to form in any sense part of that country.[8] On the other hand, the expression "ἐπίκτητον ἔθνος", which we find used to describe the Amphilochians, Acarnanians and Ambraciots,[9] seems to indicate

---

[1] Diodorus, XIX. 67.   [2] Pp. 45–6 above.

[3] See p. 38 n.4.

[4] Diodorus, XIX. 67. Apparently Glaucias had been himself besieging Apollonia: Diodorus, XIX. 70.

[5] The garrison established at Ambracia by Philip at the time of his second Epirot campaign (p. 39 above) had been driven out soon after his death (Diodorus, XVII. 3), but the city was evidently held by Cassander's son in 294 (Plutarch, *Pyrrhus*, 6) and I should suppose that it had been once more garrisoned by Antipater after the Lamian War.

[6] Diodorus, XIX. 67 and 89. The island was at this time not yet a member of the Acarnanian league.

[7] Beloch, III. 1. 291, thinks that Amphilochia formed part of the Acarnanian league at this time, although the people were not considered as Greek but rather as Epirot (Thucydides, II. 68. 5 and Polybius, XVIII. 5. 8).

[8] Except perhaps Atintania, which may well have been "τῆς Μακεδονίας", like Tymphaea and Parauaea. Cf. p. 59 n. 2.

[9] Plutarch, *Pyrrhus*, 6. Macedon had an interest in these districts which was capable of assignment.

that the relationship was not merely one of alliance between nominal equals, but that there was, even in theory, some admitted dependence, confirmed possibly by the presence in some cases of a resident (epimelete) of King Cassander[1] and of some Macedonian troops. Such a dependence would not, of course, necessarily involve any interference with the form of local institutions.

Cassander's power in North-West Greece fluctuated from time to time during the rest of his reign—largely in response to the rise or decline of the influence which the Antigonids could bring to bear in Europe, and at his death (297), though it was less than it had been seventeen years before,[2] it was still considerable. In 294, however, his son Alexander abandoned it all—and even part of Macedon proper[3]—to Pyrrhus in return for help against his brother and at one stroke doubled the strength of the Epirot king. How did this change affect the cities and peoples in question? Ambracia, we know, became Pyrrhus' capital[4], and if the presence of a Macedonian garrison had been distasteful that of the Epirot court was probably even more displeasing. The small peoples— Parauaeans, Tymphaeans and Amphilochians—were probably incorporated in the Epirot league, but Acarnania, which is our chief concern, remained outside it and there is no reason to suppose that Pyrrhus exercised a more direct control over its government than Cassander.[5]

The friendship between Macedon and Acarnania had arisen out of mutual hostility to the Aetolians. Pyrrhus—in contrast to Cassander—was from the first on friendly terms with that people and became something of a hero among them after his campaign against Demetrius in 289.[6] The position of power in northern

[1] Cf. p. 46 above.

[2] Neoptolemus, his ally in Epirus, had been forced to share his throne with Pyrrhus. Corcyra, which he had tried to capture in 300, and Leucas were held by Agathocles, while Apollonia and Epidamnus were probably either independent or under some Illyrian prince.

[3] Geographically Tymphaea and Parauaea were not parts of Macedon, but they had been held by successive kings of Macedon since about 350 (pp. 38–9 above) and were now regarded as part and parcel of that country.

[4] P. 60 above.

[5] Swoboda, *Staatsaltertümer*, p. 300 n. 1, in Hermann's Lehrbuch.

[6] *Syll.*³ 369. P. 62 above.

Greece to which he attained by 286 would no doubt, if it had
proved lasting, have resulted in a change for the worse in their
relations, but in 285/4 he was defeated by Lysimachus and so
one is not surprised to find him taking Aetolian mercenaries to
Italy[1] and still enjoying the friendship of that people at the time
of his Peloponnesian campaign in 272.[2] What, meanwhile, was
the position of Acarnania? It is possible that she used the occasion
of Lysimachus' victory to throw off Epirot control, but the
evidence on which it is sought to rest this conclusion is not to my
mind convincing,[3] and I should rather suppose that Pyrrhus' relations with Acarnania, whatever they may have been, remained
unchanged until his death. The capitulation at Argos[4] in its turn
obviously afforded Antigonus an opportunity to stipulate for the
freedom of Acarnania and so to leave the door open for a renewal of Macedonian influence there, and of this opportunity I
imagine that he availed himself. Again, however, it is impossible to be sure that Epirot control of Acarnania came to an
end.

We have now brought our sketch down almost to the "terminus
post quem" of the Aetolo-Acarnanian treaty to which I have referred and which must apparently fall after 269–268.[5] As a lower
terminus we have nothing more satisfactory than (a) the partition
of Acarnania, the date of which is—between wide limits—itself
quite uncertain, and (b) the opinion of experts that the writing of
the treaty is of the earlier half of the century. The document
itself shows Acarnania negotiating apparently as a free agent and
contains elaborate provisions for the fixing of a boundary which
in the preceding years had presumably been disputed. Further,
it appears from it that Leucas was a member of the Acarnanian

[1] Dionysius Hal. xx. 1.
[2] Justin, xxv. 4. 4. Explained by Beloch, IV. 1. 575 n. 1.
[3] It is the circumstance that Pyrrhus took Acarnanian "mercenaries"
with him to Italy (Dionysius, l.c.) from which Tarn (*Antigonos
Gonatas*, pp. 58 n., 120 n.) argues that the land must have been independent. But Pyrrhus may quite well have had recognised "rights"
in Acarnania which did not extend to disposing of the national force
in a foreign campaign of his own.
[4] See p. 86 above.
[5] Because one of the Aetolian magistrates is described as a "Dorian",
and Doris was not incorporated in Aetolia until that year. Cf. Klaffenbach, p. 224.

league.[1] Hitherto the general view has been that Pyrrhus' death had given the Acarnanians an opportunity to free themselves from Epirus and that they sought Aetolian support against any attempt of Alexander to recover his father's position. Klaffenbach, however, has now decided that both the freedom of Acarnania and the treaty date from after the defeat of Alexander by Antigonus which cannot be earlier than 264. His reasons are not to my mind at all conclusive,[2] but, while I am prepared to agree with the majority in supposing that Pyrrhus' death marked the end of Epirot control over Acarnania, I think that in their interpretation of the circumstances of the treaty they have overlooked too much the position of Antigonus. In view of past history any king of Macedon would surely be quick to take the opportunity to renew the old connection with Acarnania and in that case the Acarnanians would scarcely need or indeed, if they did, be allowed to seek the protection of Aetolia as long as Macedon was free to protect her. After the outbreak of the Chremonidean War it would be different, and it is, therefore, in the years 266 to 264 that I would date the treaty.

It is now generally agreed that King Alexander lost his kingdom during the Chremonidean War,[3] but the dates of his restoration and of the partition of Acarnania are still disputed. As to the restoration, I do not think that we can say more than that if it occurred before about 252 it came about with the consent of Antigonus and that in any event it is likely to have occurred at latest by about 250.[4] With regard to the partition of Acarnania the position is more complicated. Hitherto the general view has been that it was effected between the treaty and the Chremoni-

[1] Leucas, which had been captured by Agathocles about 300 (Plutarch, *Moralia*, 557 C) had been occupied by Demetrius about 290 and may have been recovered by Pyrrhus just before his Italian expedition; see p. 68. We do not know when the island joined the Acarnanian league, but Pyrrhus himself may have been responsible for the union.

[2] He seems to think (pp. 224–5) that the fact that the treaty did not follow immediately upon the death of Pyrrhus shows that Epirot control must have survived that event; but there is no reason for supposing that "freedom" in Acarnania would instantly manifest itself in a treaty with Aetolia.

[3] Klaffenbach, pp. 229–30. Cf. also Appendix VI above.

[4] Pp. 92–3 above.

dean War—i.e. between 268 and 266.[1] Such a date is to my mind subject to two grave objections—(a) that even the Aetolians are not at all likely to have joined with a third party in partitioning a country with which they had made a close alliance at most three years before unless there had been a greater change of circumstances than we are at liberty to assume between 269 and 266, (b) that Antigonus is not at all likely to have allowed Alexander to retain half of Acarnania after his defeat in the Chremonidean War, and yet we know that Epirus still held her half at the date of Alexander's death.[2] I feel forced, therefore, to date the partition after the Chremonidean War and Alexander's restoration—and in this I agree with Klaffenbach, though I am quite unable to follow him in his actual date for the event. As I mentioned above, he holds that Acarnania did not free herself from Epirus until Alexander's defeat in the Chremonidean War, and he further holds that the treaty with Aetolia and Alexander's restoration to his kingdom are connected, and are both to be dated immediately after that defeat. Freedom for themselves was the price of Acarnanian help in putting Alexander back on his throne and the treaty with Aetolia was a safeguard against any attempt on Alexander's part to resume his control—in the event a very ineffective safeguard, for the partition, according to Klaffenbach, followed almost at once upon the restoration.[3] This arrangement seems to me to suffer from the same defects as that which places the partition before the Chremonidean War—i.e. that it makes one event follow upon another much too quickly[4] and that it ignores the position of Antigonus. I am, therefore, led to adopt the view which I have expressed in the text, that the partition is to be dated in the years immediately after 252, when the king of Macedon was in grave difficulties.

Soon after the death of King Alexander[5] the Aetolians began to try to incorporate the western or Epirot half of Acarnania in their league by force and maintained the attempt for a number of

---

[1] Klaffenbach, pp. 225–6.   [2] Justin, XXVIII. I. I.
[3] Klaffenbach, p. 231.
[4] Curiously enough, Klaffenbach himself emphasises this objection to the current view which places treaty and partition between 270 and 266; see Klaffenbach, p. 226.
[5] See Appendix VII.

years. No help was to be expected either from their nominal suzerains in Epirus or their hereditary friend in Macedon, and the Acarnanians in their extremity are said to have invoked the aid of Rome.[1] The senate, however, provided no effective assistance and the Aetolians were on the point of completing the conquest of the land[2] when help arrived from the Illyrian allies of King Demetrius of Macedon, which enabled the remnant of the Acarnanians to preserve their independence intact. Meanwhile, however, the monarchy in Epirus had fallen for good and all.

[1] Cf. p. 97 n. 4 above.

[2] Klaffenbach (p. 232 n. 2) is of opinion that the Acarnanian city Thyrrheion, which was the arbitrator in the boundary decision recorded on the back of the treaty stone, must have been a member of the Aetolian league at the time of the decision, which he dates about 235. As he admits that Thyrrheion was Acarnanian in 231 (p. 234) he is forced to conclude that the Aetolians gained it and lost it again between 238 and 232. There is no evidence for this Aetolian reverse, and I suppose that either Klaffenbach is wrong in assuming that the arbitrator in a boundary dispute between members of a league was always a member of that league or that his date for the dispute is too early.

INDEX

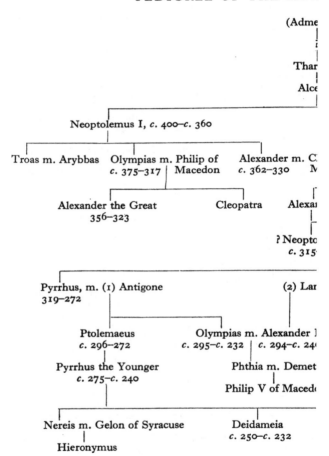

(Adme

Thar

Alce

Neoptolemus I, *c.* 400–*c.* 360

Troas m. Arybbas   Olympias m. Philip of   Alexander m. C
                    c. 375–317 │ Macedon   *c.* 362–330   N

Alexander the Great   Cleopatra   Alexa
356–323

? Neopto
c. 315

Pyrrhus, m. (1) Antigone   (2) Lar
319–272

Ptolemaeus   Olympias m. Alexander I
c. 296–272   *c.* 295–*c.* 232 │ *c.* 294–*c.* 24

Pyrrhus the Younger   Phthia m. Demet
c. 275–*c.* 240

Philip V of Maced

Nereis m. Gelon of Syracuse   Deidameia
                                c. 250–*c.* 232
Hieronymus

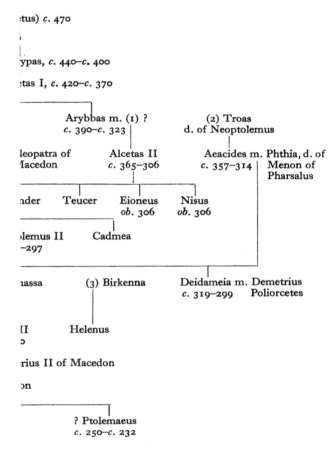

:tus) *c.* 470

,

|

ypas, *c.* 440–*c.* 400

:tas I, *c.* 420–*c.* 370

Arybbas m. (1) ?   (2) Troas
c. 390–*c.* 323   d. of Neoptolemus

leopatra of   Alcetas II   Aeacides m. Phthia, d. of
lacedon   *c.* 365–306   *c.* 357–314 Menon of
                                                     Pharsalus

nder   Teucer   Eioneus   Nisus
                  ob. 306 *ob.* 306

lemus II   Cadmea
–297

lassa   (3) Birkenna   Deidameia m. Demetrius
                             c. 319–299 Poliorcetes

[I   Helenus
ɔ

rius II of Macedon

ɔn

? Ptolemaeus
c. 250–*c.* 232

For EU product safety concerns, contact us at Calle de José Abascal, 56–1°, 28003 Madrid, Spain or eugpsr@cambridge.org.